HARVEST

HARVEST

SHORT STORIES

RICHARD SCHARINE

atmosphere press

Published by Atmosphere Press

Cover design by Matthew Fielder

Atmospherepress.com

Table of Contents

HARVEST

Every August the farmers of the Three Roads community gathered in one field after another to prepare the oats for harvest. The grain was cut and raked into rows. The men went row by row, forming the cut grain into shocks. Every man—owner, tenant, and hired—worked in every field until rows of shocks stretched from one end of the neighborhood to the other. It was a long job, but it would take at least a week for the grain to dry, and if there was no rain, the men could go directly from the preparation to the harvest.

That's where we boys came in. Three men worked at each farm where the shocks were delivered to be separated into grain and straw. (One was always the owner or tenant to supervise the unloading.) In the field there were three wagons with nine men. Each wagon drove down the field between two rows, each with a man pitching grain shocks into it. A skilled worker in the wagon used his fork to arrange the shock bundles into two rows, with the heads of grain facing one another. That way, when the worker manipulated the threshing machine feeder, less chaff got into the grain wagon. This may not be the way everyone did it, but it was our way.

The wagons were pulled by horses, driven by a young boy on the seating board. When the wagon was full, the boy drove the wagon to the farm to which the field belonged. There, two more men forked the bundles into the threshing machine feeder. It was the boy's introduction to the harvest.

But we were introduced to other things as well. At noon, we all washed together in great laundry buckets beside the farm garage and ate together at long benches. We stood together under the shade of great trees, and if the fields were damp early in the morning, huddled together next to the barn, the hired men smoking and swapping stories of experiences far beyond those of we boys.

And, gradually, we grew up.

Then the combines came and not so many men were needed. Each farm could get by on its own manpower, and because of the mechanics involved, the workers were separated from one another. The process was more efficient.

But something was lost.

Epilogue #1: August 10, 1947
(Early Morning Hours)

The Model-T crept out of the wooded hills south of the farmland. It was 2 a.m. and the road was rough and graveled, better than most but still uncertain the closer a car or wagon got to a ditch on either side. Yet that wasn't the problem this car faced. Although it proceeded down the road with an arrow-like straightness, the movements of the Model-T resembled nothing so much as the jerky leaps of a beetle feeling its way into untested territory. Or was it the skills of its driver that were untested?

The Model-T was ageless. For twenty years and fifteen million examples its operating gears remained unchanged. The last of its kind escaped from Ford's miracle assembly line two decades earlier. In this case its handler was a much newer model.

And so, the classic Model-T lurched past the farms, unnoticed by their inhabitants, desperately snatching at the rest they would need to get through another day of back-breaking labor under an unsympathetic sun.

The first farm to the west proudly announced itself as the

beginning of an empire, with the date of its founding fifty years earlier etched in three-foot-high letters and numbers on the barn. It was now occupied by the family of Henrik Temple, the youngest son of Karl Temple, and the only one of his six children living and dead to be named by his Norwegian mother.

On the same side further down was the retirement home of Karl Temple, patriarch of the clan, who had chosen to place himself where he could easily monitor the business activities of at least two of his sons. His name had no relationship to his East Prussian origins, and even less to the Poland it reverted to after the First World War, but was the garbled conclusion drawn by an Ellis Island official as Karl tried to explain his admiration for the Knights Templar. By the time he became a citizen thirty years later, the mistake had hardened into a reality.

On the west side of the road lived the family of Karl's eldest surviving son and accepted successor, Johann, or "Bert," as he was known—possibly because his older brother, Albert, who had died as a baby, had never been forgotten. Less than a year old, he lay in his bed with a case of what appeared to be a common flu. At midnight, as Karl was given to describing it at family gatherings, there came a knocking on the floor below the bedroom. The head of the household went to the basement door but found it curiously jammed.

Frustrated to find his control over his home out of his hands, Karl called out in challenge: "Take what you want, whatever you are. Take what you want and get out of my house!"

The knocking ceased—and Albert was dead before morning. Years later, when the basement floor was dug up, a man's body was found—or so the story goes.

Nine months later, "Bert" was born. Only his mother called him by his given name, and younger members of the family were known to look curiously around the room when she did so. He was as quiet as his father was garrulous. And yet they were alike in their command of a room—Karl with his language, Bert with his presence. Karl bought the land; Bert oversaw the farming. Neither had a reputation for empathy, but family was family, and to cross one was to cross them all.

There is one more farm before the road is intersected by a descending path from the east, but for reasons which will eventually become clear, we will concentrate on the Temple hierarchy.

It is at this intersection where the Model-T makes its first misstep. A few yards beyond the road climbing to the east, the car suddenly decelerates, the driver's right hand having been removed from the throttle on the steering wheel. The left hand seizes the floor-based combination clutch and emergency brake and pulls it to an upright neutral position, while the right foot seeks out the far-right brake pedal. The right hand re-connects with the throttle just in time to prevent the engine from stalling.

There is a throbbing pause as the vehicle waits while the operator contemplates options. Then the right foot seeks out the middle floor pedal, the left hand cautiously pushes the clutch forward, and the Model-T begin to move slowly backward. A car length beyond the east road it stops, and the operator reverses the procedure, pulling the clutch into neutral, pressing the left pedal to the floor, and turning the Model-T on to the road up the hill.

Was the operator now in full control of the machine? Not really. There was a near stall close to the top of the hill when the driver failed to use the left pedal to shift down into the lowest gear. Not even a Model-T could climb a hill at forty miles an hour, but sometimes a floor pedal can seem a long way away. The lesson had been learned by the time the vehicle crept past two more farms and climbed a second hill to a farm on the south side of the road—a farm, which unlike those passed earlier, had a yard light blazing from a pole at the end of the driveway, and seemingly every window in the house lit.

The Model-T coasted to a stop in front of the gas pump as the house empties in anticipation. The scraping sound of the left floor clutch moving back into its alternative identity as an emergency brake seems to free the voices of Werner Temple and his wife Peggy as they move to the driver's side of the car. The door opens and a young boy slides from the front seat to the running board and then to the ground. His parents crowd around him, uncertain whether to hug or spank. Whoever speaks is not important. The concern is mutual.

"Rickart, are you all right? Where have you been? We went back to the wedding dance to look for you! We searched everywhere. We called everyone we could think of. The sheriff's office was next! What are you doing with Jack's car? People said they saw you with him. Where is he? Why are you driving his car?"

The Model-T throbs attentively, but unhelpfully.

Day #1: August 3, 1947

Peggy McCray Temple stands at the top of the hill, the tombstones falling away in front of her like troopers at parade rest. It is the Scotch Prairie Cemetery, and she is secretary to its association, even as she is secretary to the Women's Association of the Presbyterian Church and secretary-treasurer to the local school board. She is not secretary for everything, but when someone who observes and records is needed, her name inevitably comes up. What does the secretary for a cemetery do? Sometimes she does what Peggy is doing: looking for tombstones which may have tipped over; looking for signs of animal invasion—cows taking advantage of a broken fence, the remains of a coyote's dinner, etc.; and, of course, human invasion—the remains of a teen-age beer party, for example.

Everyone deserves undisturbed rest—even the dead. And everyone living agrees; that is a woman's job.

At other times she records the newspaper obituaries of the cemetery's occupants, their names and entrance/exit dates to and from this world—recorded in a journal whose pages are divided according to family plots and their places on the hill. (Is it surprising that the people whose names are recorded here have spent their lives espousing their belief in another world in which they would be reborn in a perfect form, and yet will go to such great lengths to make sure their earthly bodies are surrounded by those with whom they had spent their lives? Perhaps, or perhaps it is the least of our human contradictions.)

If Peggy were to describe her calling, after automatically listing her community-determined categories of wife, mother, Christian, etc., she would say that she was a Witness: someone who saw the world as truthfully as possible, evaluated it according to a standard, but withheld judgment out of love and pity.

It's a calling she would have liked to pass on to the son who stands impatiently by her side.

"Mom, how much longer are we going to be? I have to go to work tomorrow."

Peggy manages to avoid a laugh. Rik is just short of nine years old, and this is his first harvest. He is simultaneously proud and anxious. He has driven the work horses before, but never when he was a cog in a full-day operation involving so many grown men. His job is to guide the grain wagon from field to bin on five farms the following week. He knows that younger boys than he have been entrusted with the task, and if he slows down the work of the men, he will be embarrassed beyond belief.

This is not feeding the chickens and gathering eggs, or even carrying pails to the milk house. This is man's work!

"Hush, young man. You knew I had to do this after church."

"I didn't know it was going to take so long," he grumbled. "Dad didn't have to go to Church today."

Peggy imagined the boy sitting restlessly in a pew, his mind imagining an adventure which she knew would become routine before the day was out. If he made a mistake, it would come later when his mind wandered to thoughts of a new adventure. Much of farming depended on the determined stoicism demonstrated by her husband Werner, who had suffered a double hernia six years earlier without ever missing a day's labor since. If he still had dreams, they never got in the way of his work. Rik was smart in school. Peggy wasn't sure she could see him replacing his father in the fields, admirable as that might be.

"Your father had to fix that wagon wheel and put a new battery in the Massey-Harris, or you wouldn't have any job to go to tomorrow. When you can do all of those things, you can decide when you go or don't go to Church. For heaven's sake, you remind me of old Mr. Johnson!"

The boy's interest flickered. "Who's he?"

"Who was he? you mean," his mother corrected him. "Mr. Johnson owned the farm just below us, next to the road. He always used to say that he wanted to be buried on the hillside with his head sticking out of the ground so he could see how the farm was doing."

Rik's eyes searched the graveyard. "Did he get his wish?"

"No, and a good thing it was too. We don't always get what we want, and it's oftentimes a good thing. You can bet his sons wouldn't have taken any better care of the farm with him watching them all the time, and you can bet they go to Church without being told to. You know what my grandfather used to say?"

"No," said the boy, still at an age when what an ancestor had said made him curious rather than bored. But his mother was already leading the way down the hill. She stopped at a familiar plot.

"There," she pointed at a thirty-year-old gravestone close to the front. "We should have put it on the stone so people would wonder what happened to him. He used to say: 'I was born in a barn, but not in a manger.'"

The boy looked puzzled. "I don't get it."

His mother shook her head in despair. "Why do we waste our time making you go to Sunday School!" Rik had already moved on to a badly worn gravestone at the back of the plot.

"This looks like the oldest stone here. Who is it?"

Peggy narrowed her eyes, hesitated, then grimly forged ahead. "That would be John McCray, and you're right. It is the oldest tombstone here. The fact the hill was empty for yards around is one of the reasons for where he was buried."

The boy's eyes were wide. "Did he want to be alone?"

"I don't think so," his mother guessed. "I think people weren't sure they wanted to be around him." She looked at Rik's face, which was silently asking the question she now knew she had to answer. "He killed his cousin. He didn't mean to. It was self-defense actually"

"He killed his own cousin!"

"Frank McCray was a mean man by all accounts. He was big, and he seemed to think that gave him the right to do whatever he wanted to. He beat up John when they were younger, and to Frank that meant his cousin was weak and deserved whatever he got. On two occasions he opened up the gate to John's farm and sent his dogs in to chase the pigs, so they got hurt, or at least didn't gain weight. The third time John grabbed a fence post and hit one of the dogs, breaking a back leg. Frank came roaring through the gateway, and John turned and hit him in the face with the fence post. He died immediately."

Rik's response was fearful and thoughtful. "What did he do then?"

Peggy spoke without hesitance. "He left the body lying in the pig yard, saddled a horse and rode to the next township where he turned himself in. He was afraid that if he stayed here, friends of John would influence the local sheriff, maybe even lynch him."

The boy looked at the tombstone. "What happened to him?"

"He was tried for manslaughter and acquitted. Some folks said that if he'd picked up the body and put it in the house, he never would have been charged. But he couldn't stay here. He moved to Iowa and lived there for the rest of his life. Still, when he died they found papers in which he asked to be buried here, and so he was all alone in this plot. But as the years passed other members of the McCray family sought him out and were buried near him. Alone so much of his life, in death he was part of a tight-knit family group."

Rik was on his knees, studying the tombstone. "I can't read the date."

Peggy knelt by her son and pulled up her sleeve to use her hand to trace out the numbers on the stone, revealing a long scratch on her arm.

"Mom, how did you hurt your arm?"

She dismissed him impatiently and remained focused on the tombstone. "Oh, your cat Theo snuck into the house, and when I picked him up to put him out, he scratched my arm."

"That old buzzard! I'll whop him!"

"Oh, don't do that!" His mother looked shocked. "He didn't mean to do it. He loves us. Sometimes things that love you can hurt you without intending to. You just have to learn to take it."

Day #2: August 4, 1947

It was eight o'clock. Breakfast was over, the chickens were fed, and the eggs gathered. Rik hurried to behind the barn where a group of working men were enjoying the first cigarette of the day. "Shall I take the horses out to the field?" he asked?

"No point," one of the men shrugged. "It'll be another hour before the shocks are dry enough to put in the wagon."

Another man glanced at the other workers, then turned to Rik, a slow smile spreading across his face. "Say kid, would you do us a favor?"

"Sure," the boy answered, eager to be of use to the grownups.

The man gestured him to come closer, and then pointed to a straw stack from earlier years. "You see that old straw stack there. We need to find out if it's dry enough to blow any more straw on it if we have to, but we're all too heavy to make an honest judgment. Would you climb up there for us and see if you sink at all?"

Without hesitating, Rik scrambled up the nearest side of the stack and moved to its center.

The man looked pleased. "That's good," he said. "Now bounce up and down there and see how firm it is."

The boy jumped as high as he could several times. "It doesn't seem to have much give."

The man turned to look at the other workers, who also grinned in appreciation. "Well, I guess it will be okay. Just slide down the end of the stack nearest the road."

Rik slid down the side of the stack, landing with a yelp in a mess of broken eggs as a dozen tiny snakes shot away in all directions. Swatting at his untouched overalls, Rik was fifteen feet from the straw before he stopped yelling.

The men roared with laughter. The one who initiated the prank took a bow and then turned to the boy. "That's a lesson for you, kid. You got to be careful before you go into a place, cause' you might find yourself in a bunch of snakes."

Rik, his head down and his face burning, walked slowly into the group of laughing men—but they didn't scatter and shoot away in all directions.

*　　*　　*　　*　　*　　*　　*　　*　　*　　*　　*　　*　　*　　*

It was the last wagon load of the field and the day, and a tired Rik urged the horses out of the field and through the gate, trying at the same time to identify an unfamiliar roaring noise. Suddenly, as the left horse climbed off the path and on to the school road, a motorcycle shot by, desperately but successfully changing its position to avoid a collision. The boy stopped the horses and stared after the bike as it disappeared down the road. His hands were shaking.

*   *   *   *   *   *   *   *   *   *   *   *   *   *

His cousin Pete's voice carried above the roar of the threshing machine. His horses waited patiently behind Rik's wagon as it was being unloaded. "I see as you were leaving the field you almost got clipped by our cousin's Harley."

"Our cousin Harley?"

Pete was only slightly older than Rik, but always seemed to have a better idea about what was happening. Rik suspected that his parents were less closed-mouth around the supper table than Rik's own. "No, Stupid. Our cousin Lawrence has a Harley motorcycle. Aunt Jean and Uncle Will's boy. I'll bet he was on his way over to see Grandpa."

"Why does he want to see Grandpa?"

Pete looked impatient, but his desire to reveal a secret was stronger. "Because of the farm! He's getting married next Saturday, and Grandpa Temple is setting him up with a farm. Probably the one over near Comstock."

"Grandpa is giving Lawrence a farm!"

Pete's eyes rolled. "He's not *giving* him a farm! He'll be Grandpa's tenant, just like your dad and my dad are. But he could *inherit* the farm, and if he does, he'll be the first one of the grandchildren to get that kind of a deal. They say it's because Grandpa likes Jill, the girl he's going to marry."

"Wow, how lucky can you get?"

"That's not the half of it." Pete was in full story telling mode.

"Grandpa likes to build the farm, but he likes to decide how the family grows too. You remember George, the guy Lu Anne married?"

"The bartender?"

"That's right. Did you know that Grandpa Temple offered George $5,000 if he'd call off the marriage and just get out of town? It was the exact opposite with Lawrence. After Jill came along, Grandpa even helped him with the payment on his plane."

"But Lu Anne and George got married anyway." Rik struggled to keep up. "The Piper Cub? What did Jill have to do with the Piper Cub?"

"Everything!" Pete's hands were moving as fast as his tongue. "When Lawrence was taking flying lessons, one of the tests his teacher gave him was a 'dead stick' landing. He'd reach over and switch off the engine, and Lawrence would have to find an empty field to put the Piper Cub down in. One day he landed the plane in a pasture right in front of a farmhouse. He taxied up to the front door, and this girl came out onto the porch. It was Jill, and three months later they were engaged!"

"That can't be true!" Rik was awed despite himself. "It's like a movie. It can't have happened that way."

Pete's certainty spilled over into anger. "It did! She came out on the porch, and he was waiting for her with the propeller still slowly circling. They saw one another and fell in love! That's the way it happened, and now they're getting married!"

"That can't possibly be true. It couldn't have happened that way."

Suddenly, the blast from the threshing machine ended in mid-roar. "Oh, for shit's sake," came a curse from the wagon. Both boys turned to see the machine belt darting along the ground as the hired man shut down the tractor engine.

Jack Rawlins swung off the Massy-Harris and began to gather up the end of the belt closest to him. "Rik," he commanded. "Pick up the other end of the belt and put it back on the threshing machine." The boy dragged the belt over to the machine and with some difficulty lifted it up to the hub. The hired man began to laugh. "Boy, haven't you ever put a tractor belt on a machine before?"

The boy shook his head in shame, but Jack was still smiling as he walked over to the hub. "Here," he said, taking the belt from Rik's hands. "You have to twist the belt before you put it on the threshing machine. That's what keeps it on the hub, and that's where the power comes from. You see," he said, demonstrating.

"Sorry.' The boy dropped his head again.

The hired man suddenly changed his tone. "Don't worry," he said. "This is your first day here. By the end of the week, you'll be an old pro."

Day #3: August 5, 1947

Now I'm a feller with a heart of gold
And the ways of a gentleman I've been told
The kind of guy that wouldn't harm a flea

But if me and a certain character met
The guy that invented the cigarette
I'd murder that son-of-a-gun in the first degree

It ain't that I don't smoke myself
And I don't reckon that it'll harm your health
Smoked all my life and I ain't dead yet

But nicotine slaves are all the same
At a pettin' party or a poker game
Everything gotta stop while they have a cigarette

Smoke, smoke, smoke that cigarette
Puff, puff, puff until you smoke yourself to death
Tell St. Peter at the Golden Gate
That you hate to make him wait
But you just gotta have another cigarette

The other night I had a date
With the cutest little girl in the forty-eight states
A high-bred, uptown, fancy little dame

She loved me and it seemed to me
That things were 'bout like that they oughta be
So hand in hand we strolled down lover's lane

She was oh so far from a cake of ice
And our smoochin' party was goin' nice
So help me cats I believe I'd be there yet

But I gave her a kiss and a little squeeze
And she said, 'Tex, excuse me please
I just gotta have me another cigarette

Smoke, smoke, smoke that cigarette
Puff, puff, puff, until you puff yourself to death
Tell St. Peter at the Golden Gate
That you hate to make him wait
But you just gotta have another cigarette

("Smoke! Smoke! Smoke! that cigarette." Tex Williams, 1947)

It was midday at the long tables and the field hands, having finished a heavy dinner, were moving on to a cigarette before returning to the harvest.

One worker patted an empty pocket. "You got a cigarette, Harvey?"

His friend reached in an overall pocket and handed him a half-empty cigarette pack. The first worker flipped the package back in disgust. "I said, a cigarette! That's a Marlboro. That's a cigarette for girls! Anybody here got a real cigarette?"

One on top of the other, the hired hands volunteered the contents of their overalls, complete with testimonials to the tobacco they contained.

"More doctors smoke Camels!"

"Yeah, but dentists recommend Viceroys."

"Call... For... Philip... Mor-ese!"

"Blow in her face and she'll follow you anywhere."

"Chesterfield Cigarettes are as pure as the water you drink."

"They must be using the cistern on this farm!"

"Reach for a Lucky instead of a Sweet, Tubby."

"Old Gold—not a cough in a carload."

The magazine- and radio-initiated commercials were reaching a hysterical peak as a late-for-dinner Jack Rawlins rode up on a John Deere- A tractor, with Pete behind, his feet on the wagon tongue and gripping the seat with his hands.

"Here comes Jack," yelled Harvey above the combined machine/shouting din. "Ask him what he smokes."

Jack switched off the engine, and he and Pete sauntered up to the table, filling their plates with gravy-soaked cold potatoes, fried chicken, and early season garden vegetables.

"You already know the answer to that," a Camel-doctored Roger Phillips commented sardonically. "Jack doesn't smoke. He doesn't need cigarettes to get through the work day. He needs to keep his breath sweet for his nighttime hobbies."

Suddenly the other men became quiet. Jack turned and walked slowly to Phillips, the dinner plate still in his hands. "Well, Rog, it must be hard to have to watch a normal man when the only sex you get is on your knees."

The other hands slowly began to form a circle around the two men, but Phillips was not so easily provoked. "Gee, Jack. The only time I ever was on my knees was when I asked a woman to marry me. Did you ever do that, Jack, or whatever your name is? I don't mean, did you ever do that with a *married* woman? Did you ever do that with a 'pure' woman?"

The two men faced one another for a tense moment. Then Phillips turned to the others, breaking the spell. "Come on, guys. We're not getting paid for dinner hour. Let's get back in the field and let everyone else catch up with us when they can."

Jack turned away, and the other field hands, except for Pete and Rik, made a quick exit. Jack looked at his plate: "Well, he's right. This food is not going to get warm with us standing here. I might as well wash the grain dust off me and get back to the threshing machine." He put his plate on a table and stripped off his shirt as he walked over to the laundry tub sitting in the shadow of the garage.

"Where *were* you?" Rik asked.

"Helping Mrs. Sturdevant get her tractor untangled from the fence." Pete's grin was as wide as his face.

Rik waited for an explanation. "What was her tractor doing in the fence?"

Pete strove to look innocent. "Well, you know Mr. Kleczkowski, who has the farm next to hers?"

"You mean the guy who does his field work without wearing any... Oh my god! Not really?"

"Not the first woman to lose control in the presence of a man's naked body," Jack commented.

The boys turned to Jack to share the joke. He was halfway through washing himself from the waist up when he realized they were staring. Jack grinned as he toweled himself down. On his right side, just above his beltline, was a hole old enough to have healed to the point that anyone could see that it would never go away.

"What's the matter, guys? Never seen anyone with a bullet hole in them before?"

Rik came to his wits first. "Where did that come from?"

"Well, that depends on what you're talking about. If you're

a doctor, that's a .32 caliber bullet wound. If it was .45 caliber, the doctor might as well be a coroner, because the victim is dead anyway. If you're a lawyer, it's something else. The victim wakes up on a bunk in the county hospital, with one wrist handcuffed to the head of the bed and a deputy sheriff sharing your room."

The boys' eyes were big.

"Ever hear of 'statutory rape'?"

Rik's face was blank, but Pete struggled for a definition. "Is that when a guy forces himself on a girl?"

"No, no, no, no!" Jack was quick to correct. "The girl can be perfectly willing. It's her birth certificate that's the problem. That and her father! She was sixteen, and I was nineteen. I think that anyone who really knew us would have argued that she was more mature than I was. She could have married me in our home state if her family had agreed. As it was, her father tracked us down parking next to a lake, blew a hole in me and called the cops.

"When I was in good enough shape to go to trial, the judge agreed with him. He gave me a choice of 'two or three,' and her father gave me a choice of his .45 or his shotgun if he ever saw me again. I never saw *her* again, although I did hear she got married a couple of years ago."

Rik regained his courage. "What's a choice of 'two or three'?"

Jack climbed on the tractor. "I'll explain it to you some time. We've got to get back to work." He paused. "Say, do you boys want to come over tonight after milking? I'll teach you how to drive my Model-T."

Day #4: August 6, 1947

The shocks of oats seemed to change color as the morning breeze swept over them. Rik put down the bucket of eggs at the fence line and took a tentative step on to the sandy loam. His bare foot made a mark, but it was shallow. The boy studied the print of his toes in the dirt. After last night's rain, the soil wouldn't support the weight of the wagons, but if the day were hot enough, the men would be harvesting again by mid-afternoon. Satisfied with his grown-up reasoning, Rik snatched up the bucket again and hurried back to the kitchen breakfast table, where his mother stood at the stove and his father and Jack were already digging into heaping bowls of oatmeal.

The man at the head of the table wore bib overalls, across the front of which could be seen a leather strap leading to that pocket watch dwarfed by his huge hand. His hair was thin enough that high on his forehead the skin, like that of his face, neck, and forearms, was tanned almost to the texture of leather, but the shirt sleeves that had been rolled up when he'd washed before eating revealed biceps that for all their size were as white as the pitcher of milk on the sideboard.

His mother caught his eye and Rik dutifully crossed to the sink, pumped water over his hands and lathered them with the coarse soap, while she loaded up another bowl with oatmeal.

"If you can get yourself fed and get some shoes on your feet by the time I take care of the pigs," his father ventured, "you can come to town with me. It's too wet to harvest this morning and I'm going to the creamery to settle the milk bill."

His mother laughed. "In that case, he'd better wash his feet too. They're growing so fast that if he's got an extra layer of dust on them, they'll never fit in his shoes, and there's nothing in the budget for new ones until school starts." Jack snorted and headed out toward the barn to finish feeding the cows. He didn't smoke, a plus in the neighbors' minds since the Katz barn one road over burned down. Their oat harvest would be stored in a neighbor's shed this year—and maybe next, unless hog and milk prices were good enough to replace the barn.

Rik's mind wandered while he waited for his oatmeal to cool. A daytime trip to town was rare, as was any town visit other than Saturday night. His parents' habits were as regular as sunrise in August. Milking was a little early on Saturday, and the family piled into the '37 Chevy for the ten-mile ride to Tripp Lake--not so risky since the end of the War and the return of tires made with real rubber—to shop for whatever could not be grown or made on the farm. Afterward, his parents would go to what they called "the movies." That is, they parked in front of the IGA and watched whoever walked down the street in front of the car. Rik could never see the excitement in that. He spent his time at one of the two "Five and Dimes," choosing the one comic book a week he could buy, and mentally calculating how many he could read and put back on the stand before the clerks kicked him out. Lately he'd been walking up to the City Library, where he could do essentially the same thing with books and be encouraged for it. On the rarest of occasions, the family would go to a real movie. On Friday and Saturday nights, the Strand showed Westerns. On Sunday, Monday, and Tuesday were the Technicolor movies with big stars that he read about in the *Gazette*, or whose story he might hear Monday nights on *The Lux Radio Theatre*. Wednesday and Thursday were gangster movies or comedies, but he never got to see them. Of course, he wouldn't do any of those things today, but it would be a change.

Rik was roused from his wool-gathering by the sound of low voices coming from the porch—voices whose tone conveyed a message not found in the words, a message he didn't understand but instinctively recognized as important. He looked up to see his mother and father exchange a silent glance. Another message. Then his Aunt Violet appeared in the doorway.

The wife of his father's brother was well-named. There was something feverish about her look, with eyes that seemed more purplish than blue, set in a face whose gold-tanned skin was framed by reddish hair in a finger wave. Her voice was girlish and teasing in a way that differed from his mother and the other farm wives.

"Jack says Yer goin' to town. Can I go with ya? The car needs a new radiator, and Henrik needs the pickup to go to the blacksmith." There was a pause. Rik's mother got an extra coffee cup from the cupboard, but her sister-in-law waved it away. "Mama needs some help in the garden," she explained.

Rik's father cleared his throat slightly. "I'm going to the creamery in Tripp Lake, not Johnsville, Violet."

"Can't ya go a little out of your way?" His aunt was smiling, but there was something in her voice that made Rik uncomfortable.

"Thirty miles is more than a little out of the way, Violet. Besides, we've all got to be back in the fields this afternoon. How would you get home? We couldn't wait for you."

"Yeah? Well, when yer right, yer right." The woman turned toward the door.

"Why not stay for a cup of coffee, Vi?" Rik's mother was encouraging. "We haven't had a chance to chat much lately."

"No thanks, Peggy. I've got to get home before the bread man comes. He's due to pick up the eggs today." And then she was gone. Out on the porch Rik heard low voices again and caught yet another glance between his father and mother.

Rik's mother hung the unused coffee cup on a hook in the cupboard. "She didn't have to walk all the way over here. That's what we've got a telephone for."

His father paused on his way to the door. "Yeah, it's right in the kitchen where she's got a husband eating breakfast."

Mother looked sharply at the boy sitting at the table, his head down, docilely focused on his oatmeal. "Little pitchers have big ears," she said.

Rik looked up. "Why is Aunt Violet always so jumpy?"

His mother pursed her lips. "It isn't up to you to pass judgment on your elders, young man," she cautioned, but was interrupted by her husband.

"Well, she wasn't always like that, Rik," he said thoughtfully. "She was fun and lively, a town girl who married a farmer and made a go of it. That's not easy, even if you've been raised for it." He looked gratefully across the room at his wife. "But with the hard times before the War and during it, things haven't been all that she planned. And in the last year or so, she's become what I call an October woman."

"What does that mean?" There was a curious look on Rik's face.

"Well, you've been around long enough to see a few Octobers," his father explained. "And your Aunt Violent had seen quite a few more. It's the most beautiful month of the year, with the clear skies and the colors in the fields and woods. But just like the harvest coming in, those skies and colors are a sign that the season is coming to an end, and no matter how crisp and beautiful the beginning of October is, you know it's going to be damp and cold by the end of the month. I think your Aunt Vi is looking at October and wondering how many nice days there are left."

"I don't understand." The boy was puzzled.

Werner Temple looked at his wife, who answered him with a verse.

> *"When comrades seek sweet country haunts*
> *By twos and twos together*
> *And count like misers, hour by hour*
> *October's bright blue weather"*

"Where did that come from?"

His mother smiled at her husband. "Oh, it's just a little poem your father used to quote to me."

The boy stared at his parents—who seemed for the moment to have forgotten him.

*   *   *   *   *   *   *   *   *   *   *   *

Rik stood quietly beside his father as he and the creamery bookkeeper went over the records. The milk plant was closed

Saturday nights, so for Rik's father (as for most farmers) the creamery made its payments whenever a break in the weather or some emergency resulted in a trip to town. After a rainy night in harvest season, Phil Chase had barely enough time for his primary job as a milk tester. Both tasks required a facility with numbers, and Chase, a short, unassuming man, was also good with people, which made him a favorite among the farmers and the members of the employment union.

In the corner of the office a girl a little younger than Rik sat at a table, intently working on a drawing. Excluded from the men's laborious checking of the figures at the desk, Rik stared at the girl, unwilling to approach without an invitation.

Phil Chase looked up from the record books and glanced across the room at his daughter. "Werner," he said to Rik's father, "it looks like this is going to take a little longer than we thought. Lynne" --he raised his voice slightly--"why don't you take Rik out to the playground by the pond, and we'll call you when we're done."

The little girl stood up and walked gravely over to Rik, took his hand and led him out the side door.

*　　*　　*　　*　　*　　*　　*　　*　　*　　*　　*　　*　　*

The playground was rudimentary, a sand box (still damp from last night's rain), a teeter-totter, and a swing set. Its primary purpose was to serve as a break for children who had come to the Creamery Pond, which also served as the town swimming pool. It was closed now because of the recent polio outbreak—three cases in town during the first month of summer. There were two types of the disease. One affected the lungs and was often fatal, while the other resulted in lifelong crippling of the legs. A side effect on this summer morning was that a young boy and girl played alone on the edge of the pond.

They faced one another on the teeter-totter, going up and down. Rik sat on the long end of the board, with the girl on the shorter end. Lynne Chase was seven, two years younger and much smaller than Rik, who had inherited his family's tendency to get their size early. She was not cowed, however, and giggled with glee when the board opposite her hit the ground and her blonde pigtails flew in the air.

Then they moved to the swings.

"Where do you go to school?" Rik caught a flash of blue eyes as they passed one another in the air.

"Plainview," he answered. "It's across the county line. I'll be a fifth grader in September."

"I'll only be in second at Eastside." Lynne was only momentarily impressed. "I'll have Miss Wells as my teacher. She's our next-door neighbor. Last year I had Miss Minogue. Who will you have?"

"Mrs. Thorne—the same as last year. She teaches everybody. But this year I move back to the big desks, and I get to raise the Flag. And I get to help carry the water from the Greenberger farm."

"She teaches *all* the rooms, even kindergarten?" There was a look of awe in the blue eyes flashing by.

Rik was astonished. "We don't have a kindergarten, and there's only one room. Every farm kid from miles around goes there, maybe as many as thirty!"

"Your dad's a farmer," Lynne said dreamily. "My dad's a milk tester. That's very important."

"What does that mean?"

"It means he's responsible for making sure there's nothing bad in the milk—nothing that will make people sick. And he decides how much butterfat there is in the milk, so that the Creamery will know how much to pay for it."

"I'd like to do that."

"You have to be very smart!" Lynne was insistent. "And very careful. He works with acid, and that can burn holes in your clothes, and in your skin. Being responsible for other people isn't easy. They could be hurt, and so could you!" She was dreamy once again. "But that's not what I'm going to do. I'm going to fly!"

"Fly?"

"I'm going to have my own airplane. And I'm going to decide where it goes," she insisted. "And I'm going to go above the clouds. I'm going to go all the way to the sun!" She turned to him. "Push me. I want to go higher!"

In an instant the boy dug his heels into the ground and halted his swing with a jolt. He scrambled behind the other swing, hesitating as he tried to interrupt its rhythm without taking a blow or slowing its speed.

"Push the swing," Lynne commanded. "Make me go higher." Rik complied with all his might. Standing far back, again and again he caught the downward arc of the swing, and with one hand on the wooden seat and one hand on the girl's slender back, he thrust forward eagerly.

"Higher," the girl screamed, as the swing elevated almost to the height of the bar to which it was attached. "Make me go higher! Make me fly!"

*   *   *   *   *   *   *   *   *   *   *   *   *

The sun was setting, and Rik was tired. He'd searched all the pasture and hadn't seen any breaks in the fence line. Still, the cow that was due to calve hadn't come back to the barn with the others at milking time, and there was still enough daylight to check the woods. He hesitated, then approached the thick stand of trees ahead of him.

The cows took advantage of the daytime coolness of the woods, and their daily presence controlled the underbrush. A few yards into the, Rik paused to adjust to the shadows around him. Off to his left was a rustle of movement, and a flash of color caught his eye. For a moment he thought his task completed, but it soon became clear that the moving image was not one figure, but two, and neither was a cow.

His Aunt Violet stopped for a moment to untangle her dress from a brier next to the path. Jack, the hired man, stood beside her, a rolled-up blanket under one arm. She reached out and took his hand, and they hurried through the clearing deeper into the trees. Rik crouched motionless, aware that he was intruding, but not sure of into what. When the couple passed out of sight into a stand of scrub oak, he rose and followed them.

Ten minutes from the field the woodland began to slope gently down into a hollow. The path became steeper, more choked. Twenty years ago, a previous owner had tried to clear the hillside of trees, and the stumps and second growth—ash, birch, chestnut, pines, firs—wreathed in parasitic mistletoe make passage and perception equally difficult. The foliage underfoot which ensured the silence of Rik's steps, also made them uncertain. The bushes that masked his presence also reached out to ensnare him. At times he lost sight of his quarry, but then his aunt's colorful dress would flash in the fading sunlight, and he would see the burly silhouette of the hired man beside her.

At the top of a ridge overlooking a ravine, he paused. Below him he could see the couple hurrying down toward a small algae-trimmed pool Rik and the other kids called "Lost Pond." Beyond it was a lean-to sometimes used for camping. Beyond that was a barbed wire fence, another section of woods, open fields, and a county trunk highway.

Rik sat down, uncertain. If he were to go further down the hill, he could easily be seen from the other side of the pond. Curiosity and shame struggled within him. He wanted to see-- and sensed that he should not. To leave the woods Aunt Violet and Jack would most surely have to come back up the hill. In this open area, there were still a few minutes of light left. Rik leaned back against the trunk of a fallen tree and waited.

*　　*　　*　　*　　*　　*　　*　　*　　*　　*　　*　　*　　*

After a time, Rik became aware of a shadow passing back and forth over his head. He looked up and his eyes caught a flash of white underpants and sandals. The long arc of a swing proceeded at a stately pace from one end of the horizon to the other, and at the point where it began its downward move Rik could see the calm face of Lynne Chase. The pattern repeated itself, and when the swing again reached its highest point, she spoke to him, in a voice curiously like that of his aunt.

"When you're ready to fly," she said. "You know where to find me."

*   *   *   *   *   *   *   *   *   *   *   *   *

Rik awoke with a start. It was night and time for him to find his way home.

Day #5: August 7, 1947

Jack sat eating with Pete and Rik at the table closest to the road on the boys' Uncle Burt's farm. He watched Burt's daughter June walk across the road to her Grandfather Temple's house. "That's a pretty girl! How old is she?"

"Sixteen," answered Pete.

"That's all I need to know." The hired man was on his feet in a flash and headed for the table furthest away, where he sat with his back to the road.

Pete laughed, sputtering potatoes in front of him. Rik didn't get the joke. He was busy watching the two tall young men talking with June in his grandfather's yard. "I wonder what Frank and Red are doing all the way over here on a workday."

Pete studied yet two more cousins the boys shared. "My guess is that Grandpa asked them to come over so he could explain why he was setting Lawrence up with a farm, and not them," he said, confidently repeating something he'd heard an elder say.

It was a possibility that had never occurred to Rik (or had never been leaked by his closed-mouthed parents). "Why does he have to do that? It's his land!

"He doesn't *have* to do anything," Pete answered seriously. "Grandpa's pretty quiet about his business deals, but he's pretty open about the way he runs his family. He thinks that if he shows you what he can do some time, the next time people will do what he wants without being told."

Much of that Rik didn't follow, so he went with his initial question. "What's that got to do with Frank and Red?"

"Grandpa figures he's already given Frank and Red a farm. Their dad went broke in the early thirties. A lot of people did. However, before the Income Tax people got there, all the cows disappeared, and about the same time the herd on one of Grandpa's farms doubled. And when the government people *did* get there with a piece of paper with Uncle Edward's name on it, he was able to show them a deed that had Grandpa giving the farm equally to him and Aunt Hilda. That meant Uncle Edward only had to pay the Tax people half, and they had to go back to court. Before the Tax people could get around to that, there was an auction and everybody who showed up only bid pennies on the dollar. Finally, Uncle Bert bought everything for almost nothing. He never took over, and the story is that he put the farm in the name of Aunt Hilda and whatever children she had. Uncle Ed was never a good farmer anyway, and so he went back to being a long-haul trucker and turned over the farming to Aunt Hilda. Frank was just a little boy, and Sandy Whitmore across the road was hired to do most of the work."

Pete paused for breath. Rik's jaw had dropped early in the story and only now recovered. "Wow, I never knew that."

Pete still had a kicker. "You see, Grandpa will do anything for his family—but only once! The next time you're on your own. And you're still missing a big point."

"What's that?" Rik's jaw was headed down again.

Pete smiled. "Have you ever wondered why Frank and Red don't look alike?"

Wordless, Rik turned to the three cousins amiably talking in his grandfather's yard. The two young men were equally tall, but Frank, the elder, had the broad body of a blacksmith, his dark eyes shielded by thick glasses, and his black hair already thinning. The same labor had left Wilson—nicknamed all his life as "Red"--whipcord thin, with hawk eyes and a mane of reddish-blonde hair. For all his life Rik had known them as brothers and at this moment could not remember ever seeing them apart.

"You still don't get it, do you?" Pete was impatient. "Frank looks like Uncle Ed. If you want to know why 'Red' looks the way he does, you should know what 'Sandy,' their next-door neighbor, looks like."

"Do they know?" Despite a life spent on a farm, Rik had never given a thought to breeding.

"Uncle Ed sure must know, but I've never seen him treat the boys differently. Maybe it's just a secret everybody's decided to keep from one another. Maybe everybody's just forgotten!"

"You don't think that's why Grandpa wants to talk to them?"

Pete clearly doubted it. "Grandpa wants the family to know that he runs things, but I don't think he wants people to know everything about the family."

Rik sat down, feeling dizzy. "How do you know all these things?"

Pete grinned. "Come to the dance Saturday night. The whole family will be there. Who knows what else I might be able to tell you?"

"My folks are going to the wedding in the afternoon. They're not going to the dance. They don't dance," Rik explained un-necessarily.

"Come with us. It's family. Your folks won't mind." Pete

sweetened the pot. "The dance is in the town square. If we get bored, we can always go to the Strand in the next block. It's Roy Rogers in *On the Old Spanish Trail*. But you're not gonna want to miss the dance."

"Why is that?"

"Lawrence is going to be playing with his own band at the wedding dance!" Pete was amazed at his cousin's unawareness of important local events. "He's the lead guitar and singer! The band plays out at the Lake Inn every Friday and Saturday night. What's more, he's training Jill to sing harmony with him. He wants them to be the local 'Lulu Belle and Scotty,' like on *The WLS Barn Dance*."

Rik looked down the road, trying to process. June was walking back home. Frank and Red had disappeared, probably into their grandfather's house. From behind the boys came a sarcastic shout: "You guys gonna get those horses and wagons out into the field, or not?"

Day #6: August 8, 1947

The last field on the home farm was done earlier in the afternoon than expected. The other workers had to pack up and go home, but Rik's father and Jack were able to start milking early. In addition to his usual care of the chickens, the boy was assigned the feeding of pigs. That completed, he wasn't required in the barn and went behind the house to play with his dog, Penny. She was less than a year old, and excited at what had been rare attention that week. Rik sat at the edge of the garbage pit and broke off sticks, which he threw down the hill for the dog to return.

It was a quiet night, and on the next road across the fields and over three-quarters of a mile away, he could hear the milking machines on his uncles' and the Rockne family's farms.

Behind him was the powerful beat of the DeLaval machines, which sat on the floor of his father's barn. Furthest away were his uncles' Surge milkers, hanging from belts on the cows themselves, high-pitched and matching in tone, if a hair uneven in rhythm. Finally came the bell-like clarity of the Universal machine on the Rockne farm.

The longer that he listened the more musical the milkers seemed. Funny that he'd never noticed it before. Maybe when he hadn't been in the barn, he'd been in the house, or maybe he just hadn't heard the sound enough times. His father could tell what field the cows were pasturing in by the taste of the milk, and in winter could discern the beauty in the pattern of frozen urine in the cow yard at the end of the barn. That sensitivity didn't come overnight, and maybe his recognition of the music of the night milkers didn't either.

Rik was thinking so hard that when DeLaval's shut down, it seemed more to him like a change in beat than an end to the milking. It was only when Jack emerged out of the darkness that he returned to reality.

"Ready for another lesson in the Model-T?"

"No, but I've got another question. When I asked what 'a choice of two or three' was, you promised to tell me sometime. Now that the harvest is over, wouldn't this be a good time?"

Jack hedged. "Actually, we've got one more thing to do tomorrow morning. We've got to unload the oats from the last wagon into the bin by the stock tank. That won't take long, but first we've got to empty the rotten grain out of the bin, and that place is bound to be packed with rats. Harvey is bringing over Rex, his German Shepherd, to help. I don't imagine Penny can join in. She's not much bigger than a rat herself," he said, scratching the little dog behind her ears.

"We can't do that until morning. Tell me about 'two or three' tonight."

"Okay." Jack sat down at the edge of the garbage pit. "But this is just between you and me. I'm only telling you now, so you won't bring up the subject in front of anyone else."

"I won't, I promise." The possibility of a secret to be kept only made Rik more eager.

"Maybe this was something that started during the war. I wasn't paying much attention until it happened to me. I was nineteen years old. In my state, for statutory rape, I could have done hard labor on the highways until I was twenty-one, and even after I was released still have a criminal record. My other choice was to enlist in the armed services for three years and maybe get killed overseas, but have all charges erased the second I was in the service."

Jack lit a Marlboro. It was the only time Rik had ever seen him smoke.

"It seemed like an easy choice to make. Maybe I'd be a war hero like John Wayne in the movies. At least if I got out without a record, I'd be able to get a job afterward. Of course, I didn't know how much I was going to hate the Army."

"Why was that?"

Jack snorted and flicked ashes into the garbage pit. "Orders. Orders for no reason at all. It didn't have anything to do with a job that needed to be done. If you did the job, they'd find something to fill the time, like moving rocks from one side of the road to the other—and then back again. You learned to make every job last as long as possible, because there was no point in finishing it. But if they thought you weren't giving your best, they'd 'discipline' you—run you around in a circle, screaming some stupid-ass chant. Make you stand for an hour with an M-1 at parade rest. They were smart enough never to give you any ammunition. It's war all right, but the enemy isn't Krauts or Japs!"

"My dad gives you orders—every day."

The hired man looked at him, incredulous. "Your dad! Your dad is out in the field with me every working hour of the day! He may tell me what to do, but that doesn't mean he isn't doing it himself. He gets me up to help with the milking every morning, but he's up *before* I am. And the work makes sense! In the field, in the barn, in the hog pen—even in your chicken house. We're working on something people can eat, or wear—use some way. On nights when I decide to drive the Model-T to town or to the tavern across the county line, I leave him sitting at the kitchen table paying bills or talking to your mother. Do you realize what a woman she is? Your father does—and he treats her that way. He may wear bib overalls and an old felt hat, but he's worth more than any officer I ever saw."

"What happened to you in the Army? Did you go overseas?"

Jack gave a short, mirthless laugh. "No, I went AWOL! Do you know what that means? Looks like I'm adding to your vocabulary as well as teaching you how to drive. It means I deserted—during war time. And it was worth it!"

What Rik was listening to was against every movie, every radio serial, and every comic book he'd read. "I don't understand," he finally managed.

Jack's face glowed in the darkness as he lit another cigarette. "We were in the infantry, so it was only right that I should walk to where I wanted to go. We spent the end of summer at Fort Dearborn in Chicago packing up equipment and our gear. On September 7th, the day after Labor Day, we started walking north-west to Camp McCoy, Wisconsin. It was 270 miles away. We were told we were going to march three miles an hour, ten hours a day, and be there at the end of nine days.

"It was crazy, of course. They'd just got done teaching us that regular marching speed was 2.4 miles an hour, and 'double-time' was 3.6. That meant we would have to have spent half the day at full trot, carrying every ounce that was assigned to us. The NCOs just carried rifles, and the officers rode in jeeps. People began falling out before the first afternoon was over, but I wasn't one of them!

I lasted six days until we were south of Madison, the state

capitol, and that night Jefferson Adams emptied his pockets of all IDs, tore all the tabs off his fatigues, and John Wilson started walking toward Milwaukee. I got five hours before I came across a farm with a haystack in it. The farmer found me sleeping there the next morning. He was an old man, and he didn't ask very many questions. It was harvest time, and the only question I remember was whether I wanted a job. He got me some overalls, and I worked there through the winter and the next spring, and I learned how to be a farmer.

"In May he died of a heart attack, I suppose, and because I wasn't in a position to answer too many questions, I started walking again—this time south. Two days later I'd eaten everything I could carry with me, and I walked up to the first farmhouse I saw and asked for a job—telling the farmer everything I'd learned at the last farm, without telling him where it was. His wife sat me down for supper, and John Wilson stayed two years. That's where I got my Model-T."

Rik sat quietly, with a sleeping Penny in his lap. "Why did you leave?"

Jack stretched uncomfortably. "Why do I always leave? There are men who appreciate their beer more than they appreciate their wives, and I was a young man. They always figure it out, though. I had my Model-T, and he had a '41 Chevy and a shotgun. Fortunately, he'd been drinking all day to gear himself up to deal with me, and he crashed at the first crossroad. I drove all night and the next day and was about out of gas when I pulled up by that gas pump over by the grain shed. Your dad needed somebody to help with planting, and Jack Rawlins has been working here ever since."

"You would never treat my Mom and Dad that way?"

"I would never treat your Mom and Dad that way, because they're not that kind of people."

Day #7: August 9, 1947 (Morning)

"I'm still not sure you're being out here is a good idea, Rik."

The boy tried not to plead. "I'll be fine, Dad. I want to help."

His mind made up, Werner Temple did what he could to assure his son's safety. "Okay, keep those bicycle clips tight around the bottoms of your pant legs. Button your shirt sleeves and your neck. Keep your gloves on and the ear flaps on your cap down!"

The boy looked at the men around him, who were following some of the precautions, ignoring others. "Gee whiz, Dad, it's August!"

"Rats don't have calendars." Werner moved on. "Roger, you and Billy shovel the old corn as far to the back as possible. Harvey, you and Jack pitch it on the wagon. The rest of you take your shovels and kill as many rats as possible. I don't want them all over the farmyard. Harvey, where's that German Shepherd of yours. I thought you were going to bring him."

"I did, Werner," the hired man apologized. "He's the best rat catcher I ever seen. I opened the door of the pickup and that was the last I saw of him. I hope he ain't tryin' to run home. He'll get lost, sure."

Werner frowned. "Well, we can't wait. You can look for him later."

The two hired men at the front of the grain bin had barely managed a shovelful before its tenants made their presence known. A large black rat, nearly the size of a cat, hurtled from a corner directly at Rik, who swung down at it with his shovel, missing it clean as it shot between his legs. At the rear of the bin, Jack's shovel backhanded it eight feet in the opposite direction, where Werner came down with the edge of his shovel and sliced it in half. A half second later a second rat skidded in the blood, and Rik, having learned his lesson, hit it with the side of his shovel, driving it airborne onto Roger's back.

There followed a dropped shovel, a string of curses and a frantic dance before Billy could knock the dying rodent loose from his fellow worker. Meanwhile, a third rat found a gap between Harvey and Jack and sprinted under the wagon and out of sight behind the hog pen—as a carefully formulated plan collapsed into chaos.

Werner grabbed Rik by the arm, shoved him out of the grain bin, and slammed the door shut, as twenty of their opponents jeered and danced in the presence of the humans' incompetence.

"Harvey, for god's sake you and Jack go find Rex! If that doesn't work, we'll surround the bin with shotguns and shoot 'em to death!" The two hired men headed around the corner toward the farmyard, with Rik behind them, striving to keep up.

* * * * * * * * * * * * *

In the midst of the dusty driveway on the other side of the grain bin, the men skidded to a halt in front of another natural, if unexpected, sight. The huge German Shepherd and the relatively minute Penny crouched back-to-back, apparently trying to pull away from their attachment to one another by a firm cord. The men were nonplussed. For the boy, however, it was another lesson in a week packed with sexual education.

"Oh, my heck," breathed Harvey.

A thoughtful look passed over Jack's face. "You've been working on a farm a long time, Harvey. Did it ever occur to you that the only animals who have sex face to face are humans?"

It hadn't, but it did trigger another possibility to Harvey. "Do you think it has to do with love?"

"No." Jack continued to stare. "But it sure would make things that aren't love a lot easier."

Harvey thought again. "What are we going to tell Werner?"

"I don't know about you," Jack turned and looked at Rik, "but I'm going to tell him we couldn't find the dog."

Day #7: August 9, 1947 (Evening)

They were early leaving for town. Uncle Henrik had started milking as soon as they got home from the wedding. Werner, with Jack apparently in no hurry to get to the dance, had followed his normal schedule, but without Rik. Aunt Violet had chattered the whole way, smoking a Marlboro, invigorated at the prospect of a celebration, and promising everyone (more than once) that she was going to take part in a way that would surprise them. Uncle Henrik was taciturn, as he usually was unless he had been drinking. Even Pete was quiet. Rik was uneasy. He was comfortable with routines and didn't like surprises. His idea of a family get together was a Thanksgiving or Christmas dinner. On a normal Saturday, excitement meant comic books in a drugstore or a "five and ten," and if there was music, it was *The WLS Barn Dance*, which could be controlled by a radio dial.

As it happened, the bride and groom hadn't arrived by the time that they did, and any band members who had, mingled happily with the small group that hadn't a chance to talk with one another after the wedding. Some were drinking, but they weren't loud, and Rik, having been raised in a tee-totaling household, relaxed. With no one else their age in sight, Rik and Pete headed for the Strand and Roy Rogers.

Rik wondered why his parents were against him going to the movies alone on a Saturday night. They didn't mind him wandering around town or going up to the library alone. A Western never lasted an hour and a half, even with previews and a short of some kind—less time than they spent at the grocery and feed stores, not to mention *their* movies in front of the IGA. Rik was nine years old. A movie cost him twelve cents, only two cents more than a comic book. If he saved another nickel, he could get a Pepsi-Cola at intermission.

The first showing of *On the Old Spanish Trail* was half

over by the time they found their seats. The action scenes were starting, but Rik didn't mind waiting through the intermission for the first half. He liked the previews and getting to know the characters who would later turn out to be heroes or villains. Roy was a hero, of course, but it said on the screen that "Rico the Gypsy was the Mexican Roy Rogers," and you could tell because he fought right alongside of Roy, and he had a girl-friend, Lolita, that he sang with just like Roy sang with "Candy Martin." Rik had seen Lolita in other Roy Rogers movies, and she always did a wild Mexican dance. He bet there wouldn't be anything like that at the wedding dance they'd just left.

Rik liked the action scenes, but his favorite came when Roy and Candy sang "*My Abode Hacienda*," a song he had heard on the radio. It was as if a plane dropped out of the sky and taxied up to a ranch house, and a beautiful girl walked out on the porch to offer her love and the ranch to the pilot.

It was perfect.

*   *   *   *   *   *   *   *   *   *   *   *   *

As they were leaving the Strand, Pete pointed at a lighted win-dow above the marquee. "That's where Uncle Ed's girlfriend lives. She works as a waitress down the street."

*   *   *   *   *   *   *   *   *   *   *   *   *

Someone had decided the dance lacked energy. Someone had decided that not enough people were dancing. Rik had entered too late to know who that someone was, but by now every-one was in a circle around the town square, holding hands and stamping their right foot. As he approached the circle, an eager dancer grabbed his hand, Lawrence began singing, the music started, and they were off.

Feudin', a Fussin', and a Fightin'
Sometimes it gets to be excitin'

Don't mind that ornery neighbor down by the creek
We'll be plumb out of neighbors next week

The circle moved faster and faster, until an elderly dancer behind Rik could no longer keep the pace and let go of his hand. He found himself whipped out at the end of the line, which resembled less a circle than a snake, which struck again and again as he strove to keep his feet under him.

Grandma', poor old grandma'
Why'd they have to shoot poor old Grandma'
She lies 'neath the clover
Someone caught her bendin' over—picking up a daisy

Four, five, six times around the Town Square at the end of the line! Rik found himself dangerously close to the bushes at the far end but stubbornly held on. Through the music he could hear circle dropouts cheering him. He looked forward to see the dancer ahead of him. It was his Aunt Vi. He missed a step!

Feudin', a Fussin', and a Fightin'
This is a wrong that needs a rightin'
Let's get that funeral service over and then
We'll go feudin' and fightin' again

In mid-shout, the cheers broke into a combined laugh and cry of concern as Rik crashed through a row of chairs at the foot of the band. People rushed to help him up, some to congratulate, some to console. Someone pushed a cup of liquid into his hand. He downed half of it before he realized its strangeness. He looked up to see Roger grinning at him. It was Rik's first beer.

*   *   *   *   *   *   *   *   *   *   *   *   *

The crowd's interest faded quickly when they determined that Rik wasn't hurt. He helped straighten up the chairs in front of the band and found himself a place further down the circle. The music started again, and a moment later Pete plopped down beside him.

"Where did you go when I was flying around out there?"

Pete protested his innocence. "I was out there too! I was just between two people who had a better grip on things. If you don't want to dance, you shouldn't be on the floor."

Rik's irritation wasn't satisfied. "Where was I supposed to go?"

Pete stood up. "Do what I always do. Go to the car. It's never locked." Then he was gone.

*　*　*　*　*　*　*　*　*　*　*　*　*

The band began to play what Lawrence announced as a "family dance." You had to dance with someone to whom you were related. Rik looked around nervously, but his relatives were otherwise occupied. In front of him his Aunt Hilda and Uncle Henrik—older sister and younger brother—took hands and moved out onto the floor to Hank Williams' "Your Cheatin' Heart."

Your cheatin' heart will make you weep'
You'll cry and cry and try to sleep
But sleep won't come
The whole night through
Your cheatin' heart will tell on you

Rik found himself concentrating on his aunt and uncle, who danced together beautifully. Why, he thought, did his father never dance? Was it his double hernia? Was his Scotch Presbyterian mother against it religiously? And if so, why did they seem so perfectly balanced in other ways?

When tears come down like fallin' rain
You'll toss around and call my name
You'll walk the floor the way I do
Your cheatin' heart will tell on you

Suddenly his muse was interrupted. Without missing a step, there was a change in his aunt and uncle's dance. Their upper bodies were tense, their faces grim. Uncle Henrik was as quiet as ever, but Aunt Hilda was speaking, and not casually. Even from this distance, Rik was aware of the emotion behind the words being spit out, although he could not understand what was said.

Your cheatin' heart will pine someday
And crave the love you threw away
The time will come when you'll be blue
Your cheatin' heart will tell on you

At that moment their dance ended. Uncle Henrik was holding Aunt Hilda firmly by the arms. What he said was short and fierce. His aunt stepped back, her face white, and sank to the floor. Rik did not move from his place, but in an instant the scene was surrounded by other dancers.

"What happened, Henny?"
"It's too hot. She fainted."
"Help me get her over a chair!"
"I'll get her some water."
"Where's Edward?"
"What happened to Ed?"

When tears come down like fallin' rain
You'll toss around and call my name
You'll walk the floor the way I do
Your cheatin' heart will tell on you

*   *   *   *   *   *   *   *   *   *   *   *   *

During intermission a play was scheduled, and the dancers grabbed chairs and formed a half circle at the far end of the Town Square. Rik looked with amazement, but the crowd had seen this before. They laughed and applauded as the cast entered. Upstage was a zoot-suited figure with an incredibly broad-brimmed hat, a fake white beard, and a tie that stretched to his knees. He carried what appeared to be a Sears Roebuck catalog.

A cheer went up. "It's Red! Ya can't hide them ears! He'll get 'em married all right!"

From the right came the "Bride," Aunt Hilda's other son, Frank, mincing bow-legged in size 12 high heels, and wearing a checkered dress which strained to cover his 220-pound bulk. A stringy wig which added to his six-foot height strove to match the coloring and intensity of his naturally hairy legs. A large, tattooed heart decorated his left bicep. He too received the audience's recognition and jeers.

But nothing could match the roar that went up at the arrival from the left of the "Groom," a good ten inches shorter than "his" mate to be—if not for a top hat whose perilous condition matched that of his loosely hanging tuxedo. The ensemble was given depth by a shock of hay, which stuck up from the rear of his tuxedo collar and tipped the top hat forward. To protect the toes which peeped from the front of his shoes, the Groom used a barn broom to vigorously sweep the path leading to the bride.

"Vi! Vi! Vi! Vi! **VI!!!**," the crowd chanted.

"Show 'em some balls, Vi!," suggested a bass voice, immediately shushed by his wife.

The "minister" took charge. "I can see why you two are getting married at night." He flipped open his catalog. "I was going to give you the short service before you sobered up. My girlfriend called me and said, 'Come on over. There's nobody home.' So I went over. There was nobody home. So I'm giving you the long service."

"I'm supposed to marry that?" The "Bride" pointed at the "Groom." "I don't like his looks."

Immediately, her mate-to-be picked up the broom and commenced to whack the bride top to bottom on both sides to the cheers of the crowd.

"Cease and desist," commanded the Minister. "Save it until you get home where it's perfectly legal. As for his looks, I married my wife for her looks, and now I don't like the looks she's giving me. That's why I go visit my girlfriend."

"But he's beating me up," the bride protested.

"That's only because I insisted he be sober for the wedding," the Minister explained. "Ordinarily you'd be fine."

"You mean he'll be drunk all the time?"

The Minister looked disgusted. "That's your fault! If you weren't so ugly, he wouldn't have to be drunk to go to bed with you."

"Wait a minute!" The bride raised a hand. "If he keeps beating me, won't he hurt my twat?"

"Never put a question where God put a period!"

This time the laugh was uneasy. One voice said just loud enough to be heard: "I don't get it," followed by a much louder laugh.

The bride protested again: "Wait a minute." The Groom cocked the broom like a determined batter with a 3-2 count. The bride winced. "Never mind."

The Minister looked satisfied. "Good. Let's get on with the ceremony. Will the Bride and Groom please join hands? Sir, please move your broom to your left hand." He sighed. "Reflecting on what marriage means is my favorite part of a wedding. My wife and I were happy for twenty years. Then we met. For her birthday, I wanted to surprise my wife by turning the bed into a trampoline. She hit the roof. I asked my wife what she wanted for Christmas. She said that nothing would make her happier than a diamond necklace. So I got her nothing. Our doctor told my wife she should never again touch anything alcoholic. Now she's filing for divorce."

The bride growled. "Where did you get all those terrible jokes?"

The Minister flipped open the catalog. "Amazing what you can find on sale in Sears and Roebuck."

The Groom was on him with the broom in an instant, whacking off his beard and his hat, and unloading on his buttocks when he bent over to pick them up. The bride moved in, but the Groom caught him on the back swing, and he did a complete somersault. She stood between the two of them, swinging back and forth, breathing heavily, moving from head to foot, from cheek to chest.

The audience cheered and chanted: "Vi! Vi! Vi! Vi! **VI!!!!**" The two men leaped to their feet, and taking the Groom by her hands, took several steps forward and bowed, first downstage, then to the left, then to the right.

Directly opposite them, Henrik began to move forward. Violet looked up, her expression changed, and breaking free of her fellow actors, turned, and sprinted toward the upstage darkness. Henrik followed her, breaking into an unsteady trot, but the two brothers closed the gap between them. Red and Frank, younger than he—and bigger. Henrik paused, his eyes on the wall, not the prey. The chase was over.

* * * * * * * * * * * * *

It was the last number of the Wedding Dance, and the treat that had been hinted at was fulfilled. Jill came from her place behind the band and stood at the microphone with Lawrence, to sing the popular favorite of the *WLS Barn Dance*'s Lulu Belle and Scotty, *Have I Told You Lately That I Love You?*

> *Have I told you lately*
> *That I love you*
> *Could I tell you*

Once again somehow
Have I told with all my heart
And soul how I adore you
Well darlin' I'm telling you now

Rik watched the couple at the mike. Everything about them seemed so perfect. Their harmony, the way they looked at one another. Tomorrow they would go on their honeymoon—not to some normal place like the Wisconsin Dellswhere his parents had gone. They would take off in Lawrence's Piper Cub and fly. (Where had he heard that idea before?) And when they came back, they would land on their own farm and make a life together that have didn't the problems other couples have.

My world would end today
If I should lose you
I'm no good
Without you anyhow
This heart would break in two
If you refuse me
Well darlin' I'm telling you now

Rik broke off his wool-gathering and looked around at the dance floor. Between the couples who seemed as entranced as he had been, he saw his Uncle Henrik, not dancing, but sliding between the dancers, scanning the Town Square with an intensity that went unnoticed in the dream-like atmosphere created by the ballad. Rik knew immediately what he was searching for and why he didn't want to be questioned. He tried to blend back into the darkness.

Have I told you lately
How I miss you
When the stars
Are shining in the sky

Have I told you why
The nights are long
when you're not with me
Well darlin' I'm telling you now

His uncle shook him by the front of his jacket, and his shirt came free of his trousers. "Where is she? *Where is she?*" Rik didn't know, but for some reason he was unable to answer. He knew something, but it wasn't anything he could share!

Suddenly he realized he was free—scrambling over the stone wall leading to the parking lot. *The Car!* Isn't that what Pete said? It would be safe in the car! If only he could remember where it was in the parking lot. The 1946 Buick Roadmaster? It should stand out amid all the prewar, many times repaired substitutes for modernity! And there it was! In front of him, and with Uncle Henrik nowhere in sight!

But somebody else was.

Behind the Buick, her hands grasping the trunk handle, was his Aunt Violet, leaning over, with her skirt pulled halfway up her back. Behind her, holding firmly onto her hips, his trousers down around his ankles, Jack pumped away frantically.

Day #8: August 10, 1947
(Just After Midnight)

The Model-T throbbed its way through the back roads from Tripp Lake to the neighboring county, but its riders were silent the whole way. Rik sat as far to the right as possible, dreading any explanation of the evening that might be available. It was finally Jack who broke the silence.

"I won't be here when you wake up in the morning. I doubt

that there's anything I could say to your parents that would make them want to keep me around, and there's nothing that happened that I'd want to tell them anyway. They'll get the gist of it sooner or later." He cranked down one of the windows and threw away half a pack of Marlboro's.

"Where will you go?"

"Across the border into Illinois, I reckon. I filled the gasoline tank before I left after milking. That ought to get me farther than anyone will want to look—to a farm in the West or an industry job in Chicago. I used to know my way around there."

Although he wouldn't have known what to call it, Rik sensed the irony. "You had a home with us."

"Not really. Only someone like your dad has a home—a place where he can watch his crops and his children grow year after year and share it with your mother. I'll never have that. I'll just have somewhere where I can rest for a while and satisfy my appetites."

"I'll miss you."

"Don't do that! Listen to your mother and grow up like your father. Or do like your cousin and wait for the music to tell you when to fly away."

Rik thought for a moment. "Maybe I will."

The Model-T tackled the low hills on the road that preceded the Temple farms. Both the man and the boy were quiet, their thoughts sheltered by the darkness of the trees that surrounded them.

Until the darkness was gone—

*   *   *   *   *   *   *   *   *   *   *   *   *

Ahead of them, and on either side, were cars—six of them! Their headlights trained on the road! The Model-T had just topped a hill when the lights came on simultaneously. To back up the hill would have been pointless. The cars on the side could have cut them off; the cars in front could have caught them.

Maybe a dozen men surrounded the cars, a few of them armed—deer rifles, a couple of shotguns. Rik recognized most of them; no one attempted to hide his identity.

"Get out of that piece of junk, you son of a bitch!" The voice of his Uncle Henrik was no surprise.

Jack slipped quietly out of the Model-T, momentarily keeping the door in front of him in case there was a shot. "You may think of me what you will, Henny, but I'd appreciate it if you didn't insult my car. Are you going to shoot me now, or are you just showing off for the neighbors?"

Henrik Temple stepped out in front of a headlight, his face in shadow but his body showing the firmness of decades of farm labor. "Don't worry about the Model-T, Jack. When this is over, it's going to look pretty good in comparison to you."

In a second, Jack cut down his odds. "By that I take it that every loser in this little circle is going to have his crack at me, not just you."

Henrik took a sharp step forward, then stopped. "No, you bastard! I don't want to share the pleasure of kicking the shit out of you with nobody! Suppose you stop hiding and come out here into the road!"

Jack was on him before the other men could react—blocking Henrik's haymaker, snapping his head back with a left, and dropping him to his knees with a right to the mid-section. He danced in front of the older man like a professional fighter. "It looks like I'll be keeping my shit a little while longer."

Back on his feet, Henrik charged, wrapping his arms around the other man's waist. Jack brought his clenched fists down on the farmer's back, but Henrik kept moving forward as Jack fought for footing on the gravel road, finally catching his heel on the edge of the ditch and tumbling over backward. Henrik straddled the hired man's chest, driving his right fist again and again into his face until it came back bloodied. Jack forced his knees up between Henrik's legs and tipped him over his head, almost immediately gaining his feet.

It was at this moment that Rik heard a loud click, the sound of a shotgun being cocked. He leaped out of the Model-T, headed for the circle but was caught in less than three steps. He looked up. It was Roger, the only married man in the work crew.

Jack also heard the click and read its meaning. He gave the rising Henrik a powerful push that sent him sprawling and leaped toward a gap between two of the other men that led to the woods beyond. One of them stepped in his path. It was Harvey, his best friend among the hired men. They struggled, and quickly two others were on him, sending him staggering back into the circle, where Henrik met him with a strong right hand to the head.

Jack was on the gravel only an instant before he was up and sprinting toward another opening. This time a rifle butt sent him reeling back in Henrik's path, where he was knocked down yet again. The farmer was breathing hard, pounding the man underneath him. With a tremendous effort, Jack threw him off and was on his feet once more, headed directly toward Rik and Roger.

When he saw what was in his path, Jack stopped. Just in time for Henrik to land a smashing blow to his kidneys. Jack wheeled around—very slowly it seemed to him. The other men had tightened the circle. There was no opening to be seen. Henrik knocked him down. When he rose to his knees, there was gravel stuck to the blood on his face—very near the spot where the farmer now kicked him. Henrik, exhausted, staggered over to where the body lay on its back. He raised a boot over the face—and brought it down.

*   *   *   *   *   *   *   *   *   *   *   *   *

Jack lay in the road, his head propped up by a cushion from the Model-T. Rik crouched beside him, clumsily attempting to clean the dirt from the cuts on his face. He had seen something like this before—when the horses had pulled his father's corn planter through a barbed wire fence. Maybe because his father had been in charge, that had seemed less drastic.

Jack sat up and Rik adjusted the cushion behind him. "I'm all right," the hired man said. "My nose is broken, but nothing else that needs fixing." With the boy's help, he managed to get to his feet and moved over to sit on the running board of the Model-T. He was breathing hard but beginning to take charge of the situation. He took the towel from Rik and held it to his nose to stop the bleeding.

Rik sat down on the cushion next to the car. "Why didn't you fight him? The boy dipped his head in embarrassment.

The man gave a short laugh and then winced because it started the bleeding again. "Who do you think was out there? The Man in the Moon?"

"You could have beat him," Rik insisted. "You're younger than he is. Faster. You look like you've been in a fight before. He didn't."

"Sometimes you have to know when to take a beating and when not to."

Rik was angry. "That doesn't make any sense! Why take a beating when you don't have to?"

Jack was surprisingly patient. "How many men were in that circle?"

"I don't know. Twelve? Fifteen?"

"And how many had weapons? Hunting rifles? Shotguns? And if I started winning that fight, how many would have used them?"

"None of them! Nobody would have shot anybody. They're not crazy!"

"Eleven of them wouldn't have shot anybody. Fourteen wouldn't have shot anybody. All it takes is one. That was a mob, Rik. Yesterday, Harvey was my best friend. Tomorrow he might be my best friend. Hell, tomorrow Henny will be back together with Vi, and what happened tonight will never come up again." Jack stood up to see what was functioning and what wasn't. "Let me ask you one more question. Where were you during this fight I was supposed to win?"

Rik was amazed. "You know where I was! In the circle, right across from you!"

Jack nodded his head. Some places on his face were beginning to swell, but his nose had stopped bleeding. "One more good reason not to have bullets flying around. Now, put the cushion in the back of the Model-T and drive home. Werner and Peggy will be frantic by now."

"Me? *Drive* home! Where are you going to be?"

"As far south as I can get before daybreak. Hopefully, the state highway. Although with the state of my face and clothes, chances of getting a ride are pretty poor." Rik looked at him, incredulously. "I already told you that I'm through here. What happens in this part of the country if someone named Temple files charges against me? What happens if somebody gets hold of my military record? My only hope is to start over. To not make the same mistakes. I can't do that here."

"Dad would stand up for you if he knew what happened."

"There's no point in me coming between your dad and his brothers." Jack took a jacket from the Model-T and slipped it on. Out of the pocket he took a driver's license with the name, 'John Rawlins,' and tore it up. "No way of hiding a Model-T, either. Maybe your dad can get something for it." He looked at Rik, who had tears in his eyes. "You saw everything that happened this week, but you don't understand it—not really. When you do, learn from it. Fly away, like your cousin."

*   *   *   *   *   *   *   *   *   *   *   *   *

Down the road, a tall figure disappeared into the darkness as a boy searched a Model-T for a starting crank.

Epilogue #2: August 10, 1947
(Mid-Afternoon)

Rik sat under the trees in his grandfather's flower garden, idly leafing through a comic book. Who took care of the garden, he wondered. His grandfather had never shown any interest in a crop that couldn't be harvested. It had been the hobby of his grandmother, who had died two years ago in the spring. He remembered being brought to the house at three in the morning, along with the other nearby grandchildren, to see her before she passed. He remembered how hard she breathed.

The reason his father was here this time had to do with the harvest. The supposition was that tractor-drawn combines would replace the horses and wagons. The brothers and their hired men would still work together, but the rest of the neighborhood were on their own. At any rate, that's what Grandfather Temple and his sons were to discuss this afternoon.

Why was Rik there? Certainly, his opinion wouldn't be asked. He hadn't been up long, had actually just finished breakfast. The events of the preceding night and the absence of Jack hadn't been mentioned. His dad had done the milking and all the chores. Rik couldn't imagine those circumstances lasting long. His mother had suggested he accompany his dad in the '37 Chevy because Lawrence and Jill were supposed to drop by on the way to their honeymoon. The Model-T sat quietly by the gas pump where he'd left it.

Werner was the first of the brothers to arrive. His Uncle Burt walked down the road and nodded to Rik as he went into the house. In the opposite direction Uncle Henrik powered up in the '46 Buick Roadmaster, and though he must have seen Rik, gave no sign as he parked in the driveway and entered by the front porch entrance.

None of the wives had been invited.

Left on his own, Rik returned to his comic book. It wasn't

his, which invariably was a Disney publication like *Donald Duck* or a Western like *Roy Rogers*. Pete, who was able to get away with more racy choices, had lent it to him. *Nyoka, the Jungle Girl*. The plot really wasn't that much different than a Western—bad guys stealing from good guys. Only in this case, the good guys were black natives who spoke pidgin English and the bad guys wore pith helmets instead of Stetsons. The difference was in Nyoka herself, who was slim with long brown hair and red shorts that she wore as high as possible. Sometimes she swung through the trees like Tarzan. She was inevitably captured, but always figured out a way to escape.

A roar caught Rik's attention, and he stood up, looking down the road for its source. For a moment he thought it a motorcycle—until a Piper Cub appeared low in the northern sky. Lawrence and Jill weren't "dropping by" on their way to their honeymoon; they were merely making their presence known.

The little plane passed over the house, banking sharply over Uncle Henrik's farm further to the South and reversing its path. The four patriarchs of the Temple family appeared on the front porch and spilled out on the lawn, as if to pay tribute to the next generation. They waved and the Piper Cub banked again, its controls now in other hands. Jill was learning to fly. Lawrence opened the door on his side, leaned out, and waved: "Bye, Grandpa! Thanks for everything!"

The plane righted its path and returned to the North—an artwork that knew when to make its exit. The men on the lawn continued to wave until it disappeared, as if reluctant to return to their self-assigned task.

Rik stayed quietly in the garden, making no attempt to be seen. As he watched the Piper Cub under the command of a family-approved hero, with his own farm, his own band, his own motorcycle, and a beautiful bride, in his mind it dissolved into the image of a man walking down a tree-surrounded road, looking up with wide-open eyes at an arching swing containing a slim young woman with long brown hair and red shorts.

THE PEACEMAKER

We try to get down to Sacramento to see our grandsons three or four times a year, but the best they can do to visit us is a week between camps in mid-summer. It's understandable, I guess. Mike is ten years old, and Douglas is eight, and the high plains of Oregon aren't particularly kid friendly. Pat and I have taught them riding, but they're of the video game generation and I married late, so there's what you might call a cultural gap between us. Thank God for satellite TV, or there wouldn't be anything for us to share in the evenings. Mostly we watch *NCIS*, which seems to be on about every channel, but for some reason this evening we were watching a PBS documentary on early television westerns.

Mostly the program focused on what they called "adult" westerns—*Gunsmoke, Wagon Train, Rawhide, Maverick, Cheyenne*, and the like. According to "This Was the West That Was," there were twenty-six on the air in 1959. But, hell, Matt Dillon started on radio, and so did The Lone Ranger and The Cisco Kid. Even Roy, Gene, and Hoppy had radio shows, but still I was surprised to hear a mention and see a couple of stills of Amos Stone and the Hard-Luck Kid.

"See that!" I piped up before Pat could stop me. "I was on that one." The boys brightened up for a few minutes, but they never returned to that show, and it was bedtime by the time the documentary was over. By morning, Mike and Doug had forgotten all about any outburst by their grandpa.

But I never will.

*   *   *   *   *   *   *   *   *   *   *   *

It was called *The Peacemaker* and started as a syndicated radio show after the War. When it went national in 1948. they needed a name actor for the lead, and the part went to Kirk Stevens, who had been around for a decade or so but had fallen on hard times. It was a typical "kiddie western" of the period, with the star pitching breakfast cereal and featuring a character actor with a high-pitched voice playing a teen-age sidekick. Every episode there was a new set of rustlers, or claim jumpers, or bank robbers to be brought to justice. Nobody seemed burdened with an ordinary job. After the first season Stevens put together every penny he had or could borrow and bought the rights to the show, and began to adapt it for grownups, giving everybody in the cast a backstory that would explain their specific skills or building episodes around someone showing up from the past, and so forth. During that year, he spent all his off hours actually learning the hero's skills—riding, roping, shooting, etc.

In 1950 Stevens brought *The Peacemaker* to television. That's where I come in, but my ties to Kirk Stevens went back much further.

*   *   *   *   *   *   *   *   *   *   *   *

If you're a connoisseur of "B-movies, you might remember Kirk Stevens from the *Andy Hardy* films of the late 30s and early 40s. He played Mickey Rooney's college-attending-older brother, and if he didn't get the attention that some of the girls, like Judy Garland, Lana Turner, and Esther Williams, who got their starts in this series, did, he was noticed by somebody very important—Mickey Rooney himself. Andy Hardy made Mickey a star. He was on the cover of *Time* magazine in 1940, and that can be pretty heady for a twenty-year-old. Unfortunately, Mickey read the "trades" as well, and what he was seeing was a lot of space devoted to Kirk Stevens.

You'll remember that in the movies "Reid," Andy's brother,

was always being held up by Judge Hardy and the rest of the family as a model for Andy. Andy was 5'3" tall, with a face that could get laughs, while Reid was 6'2", handsome, a star athlete and pre-law student who was always given the reasonable but sympathetic speech that explained to Andy what he *should* have done rather than get into the mess he was in now. That's okay for the movies, but the trades magazines (in Mickey's eyes) were confusing celluloid with reality, to be assuming that the relationship in real life was the same as in reel life. The final straw came when *Photoplay* ran an article suggesting that Kirk was giving Mickey tips on his love life, which inevitably was a mess on screen.

That's when Mickey started an off-screen campaign to have "Reid" written out of the series, sent to an out-of-state law school or something. The studio was shooting *Andy Hardy's Double Life*, the twelfth film in this very lucrative series when Mickey gave an interview that he was getting tired of the character and hinted he wouldn't be available for any more Andy Hardy films.

Just then, fate stepped in—not in the wisdom of Judge Hardy, or the voluptuousness of Lana Turner or Esther Williams, but in the form of a real surprise attack: Pearl Harbor. The studio had its way out. It could fulfill its star's demand, appeal to patriotism, and hype the box office, all at the same time. This movie would end with sending Reid off to war—on screen.

Andy Hardy's Double Life tried to have it both ways. The first ninety or so minutes was what a writer on *The Peacemaker* explained to me as "schlock comedy": The central character wants something, pretends he's something other than he really is in order to get it, digs an impossible hole for himself as audience anticipation builds, is exposed and laughed at, and then is welcomed back into the fold because he's basically a nice guy with whom we all identify.

Then things changed. Aunt Millie (who wasn't in the room during the reconciliation scene) comes in all upset to tell everyone that there's something on the radio that they have to hear. The family gathers around the set in the living room, and the announcer introduces President Roosevelt, who for some reason gives the speech that actually wouldn't be heard until the next day. You know the one—"a day that will live in infamy"?

Reid gets up and quietly walks out of the room. The camera pans slowly across the concerned faces of all his family members, ending with Andy. There's a moment of indecision, then Andy leaps to his feet and rushes out in search of his brother.

Reid is standing in the back yard, looking up at the stars in a medium shot. Andy walks into the frame and looks up at his big brother.

"I've got to go." Reid is still looking up at the stars.

"Where?"

"Over there. I've got to go over there—while it still *is* over there."

"I don't understand."

Then Reid gives "the speech." How do I know the way it was done? Because the writer who wrote the scene told me about it.

Reid turned to his brother and did his lines in a single, uninterrupted take. There are reaction shots from Andy in the final product, but those were inserted later.

"Look, Andy. This isn't something I want to do. What I want to do is stay in school, get my law degree, find some girl I love, settle down and raise a family like Dad and Mom—maybe in this house, or at least in a house like it. But this isn't the only house on the street. There are hundreds of others in this town, and millions all over America. And in every one of them has a family like yours and mine—folks that love one another and want to see their kids grow up to be safe and happy. That's more important than what just one guy wants. I'm going over there—and thousands of other guys will too. Because we know that we don't deserve to be happy if we're willing to risk the safety and happiness of our families, and a million other families like them. Don't you see, Andy? This is what it means to be an American! We're all one family, and when anyone in that family is threatened, we have to stand up and face that threat, just as if we were protecting Mom or Sis or Dad."

"Can I go with you?"

Reid puts his arm around Andy's shoulders. "Not yet. Some day you may have to. You'll know when the time comes." They look up at the stars together, as the theme rises and the camera pulls back away from them, up into the sky. The two young men dissolve into the lights of the house, then the street, then the town, and finally we see the lights of dozens of towns all over the country, and they don't look much different from the stars we find ourselves among as the screen dissolves into the credits.

You can buy the whole series on DVD these days, but I've been told that *Andy Hardy's Double Life* ends when the comedy plot is resolved. The rest was snipped off in the 1950s when the Powers That Be were releasing it to television and thought the final scene was "too collective."

Still, it had an effect in its time.

*   *   *   *   *   *   *   *   *   *   *   *

Andy Hardy's Double Life was released in March 1942, and it took about a month to reach the High Plains of Oregon. My father and mother saw it at the movie house in a nearby town on Saturday night, April 25th. I was mad because they left me at home with my grandmother. I was nine years old.

The following Tuesday morning, April 28th, my father enlisted in the Army.

His name was Henry Riley, and he was twenty-seven years old. He and my mother Millicent (who I never heard called anything but "Peggy") were married at seventeen, the day after she graduated from high school. You might think a wedding at that age had something to do with me, but I was born a full year later. Getting married as early as possible was pretty much the norm in rural Oregon in those days. Pop dropped out at sixteen, (the age until which the law required you to stay in school) and worked full time for his father. After the wedding, they spent a week in Portland and on the coast, and then Mom moved into Pop's room. As soon as they turned eighteen and were legally adults, they took out a joint homestead of a section of land and a month later I was born in the sleeping space of a lean-to that the family helped Pop put up. My name is Henry Riley, Jr., but everybody calls me "Hank." It's even on my IMBD.

Am I certain that Reid Hardy's speech at the end of *Andy Hardy's Double Life* was the reason Pop joined the Army? Well, that's what Mom said, and he was still talking about it in his last letter, which didn't even arrive until he got home.

Henry Riley had a Battle Star and a Purple Heart, but he threw them away as soon as the War Department sent them in the mail. That's something else Mom told me. I never saw them, and Pop never talked about what happened during "Operation Tiger."

Pop never became the hero that Reid Hardy envisioned for him, the brave warrior standing between an implacable enemy and America in the form of Mom and me. The 4th Infantry Division assigned him to the Quartermaster Corps, and that's where he stayed for the time prior to the lead-up to D-Day. Even then he wasn't to be in the first wave of the invasion but was scheduled to land with the troops that were to support the actual fighters.

The assault on Omaha and Utah beaches would have been logistically difficult enough without one of the best militaries in the history of the world trying to kill you as you did it, so Eisenhower and the Brits decided to stage a practice run on the south coast of Devon as a warm-up. The landing place for

Operation Tiger was the Slapton Sands in Lyme Bay, and zero hour was just after midnight on April 28, 1944, two years to the day after my father joined the army.

Eisenhower quite reasonably felt that troops might function better during the real thing if they'd already experienced bullets flying over their heads during the training session. The British were to shell the beach until the infantry was ready to land and stop then, so that the Americans would have the sight and smell of a devastated landscape while remaining unharmed. It was only here that the Americans and the British discovered they weren't on the same wavelength—literally! Three hundred landing crafts descended on Slapton Sands from the English Channel, and American soldiers charged up the beach into a continuing onslaught from the British guns. American and British radios proved not to be on the same frequency, and three hundred men were dead before the problem was discovered.

That was only the beginning.

The British were also unable to supply destroyer escorts for the American Landing Ships (LSTs), carrying tanks, amphibious trucks, jeeps, heavy engineering equipment, and the engineers, chemical and quartermaster troops to operate them, which were to follow the original invasion force. And here Fate played a particularly nasty joke.

Nine German torpedo boats out of Cherbourg, France, making a routine tour of the Southern English coast, came across eight unarmed LSTs, their unprotected afts exposed. Within minutes, four were hit by torpedoes, three seriously. The LST-531 sank in less than six minutes, with all its troops trapped below deck. The LST-289 had its stern blown away but managed somehow to limp into port. Henry Riley was aboard the LST-507. The torpedo that started the fires which forced the ship to be abandoned also shattered my father's left leg and seared the left side of his face beyond recognition. He wasn't conscious when one of his shipmates fitted him with a life jacket and threw him overboard, but he did come to in the icy water long enough to appreciate that his savior had fastened the jacket under his arms instead of around his waist as many of the less experienced soldiers had. In their cases. the floating devices had lifted the middle of their bodies high, while they fought to keep their faces out of the water until the freezing cold exhausted them. When the sun rose the next morning, the LST-515 returned in search of survivors, and a sailor looking out over the water remarked in awe, "You could have walked like Jesus all across the Bay just by stepping on the dead bodies."

My father was one of seventy or eighty men pulled out of the water alive. The number of those who died is just as approximate, but one count says 551 soldiers and 198 sailors. Add that to the dead on the beach and the total is easily over a thousand—more than died five weeks later on D-Day itself. My father left behind his leg that night, but the dead were always with him. I heard him scream to them many other nights, but their absence as men or their presence as demons was never mentioned during the day.

I was eleven years old, and when we heard that he was coming home, I couldn't think of anything else. I realize now that my mother was trying to tell me not to expect too much, but I didn't pay any attention. I went through the rest of fifth grade that spring in a daze, worked all that summer in the fields beside my mother, making lists in my head of the things we would do together when he arrived. It was September and time for school again when the man the Army called Henry Riley, Sr., was dropped off by a khaki-colored car with sorry-looking flags on the front bumpers.

But my father never came home.

Eventually Pop was fitted with a prosthetic leg, but he never followed through on the plastic surgery the Veterans Administration once promised him. He had some sight in his left eye, which lay in his face like a blue pool in a dormant volcano pit. He learned how to work the clutch in the pickup truck with his artificial foot, and was able to do some work that way, but the horse-drawn farm machinery was beyond him, and he didn't show much interest in the homestead anyway. Today I suppose they'd call what he had PTSD. All I knew was that he never talked to me during the day, drank as much beer as there was in the house during the evening, and screamed at dead men during the night. After a while, I slept right through it.

It was my mother who found a way to keep the family alive when the plowing, planting, and harvesting of crops got to be too much for us. The land wasn't that great for growing anything but grass, but the view was great on the Oregon High Plains, and the combination was an economic boom for some people in the post-war era. Horse farms and Dude ranches sprang up everywhere, and we provided a place for some of them to graze their stock. I was a natural with horses, and Mom wanted to encourage me to stay home. When I was in high school, she took a loan out on the homestead, and by the time I was sixteen in the spring of 1949, I was breeding and raising my own quarter horses and leasing or selling them to any Dude ranch that would come and get them.

That spring, I followed my father's example and dropped out of high school. That fall, Mom was diagnosed with cancer. It was a long winter, and she died in April—not the 28th. Fate isn't that neat. Pop and I were left with the homestead—two separate people with the same name living in the same place.

That's when I heard that one of the less successful Dude ranches in the area had been bought out by some movie people.

*   *   *   *   *   *   *   *   *   *   *

Kirk Stevens' war had been a lot more successful than my father's. Impatient with the slowness of the American military, he went north, and through the Canadian Air Force, joined Great Britain's Eagle Squadron. There were initially six American pilots who enlisted, and by the end of six weeks of combat, he was the only one still alive. While in England, he met the daughter of a senior RAF officer and they became lovers, an affair that ended tragically when the ship in which she was crossing the English Channel was torpedoed by a German U-Boat. It was tough, but the "Battle of Britain" was still going on, and he was soon back in the air.

Of course it was only a movie, but *Eagle Squadron* was cited for helping Americans understand what the English were going through, and it made a profit of nearly $700,000, which was huge in those days. The films that followed it didn't do as well.

Stand By For Action was a Navy picture in which Kirk was a spoiled playboy, who because of an administrative mistake finds himself the executive officer of a recommissioned, obsolete World War I destroyer. The film had a hard time deciding whether it was a drama or a comedy, what with two pregnant women and twenty children on board, and Walter Brennan wandering around, unable to figure out just what war he was in. Still, the Japanese battleship was blown up, and although the critics didn't like the movie, enough of the audience did.

In *We've Never Been Licked*, Kirk was an overage army brat who goes to Texas A&M to play football and unwittingly falls in with Japanese spies who are there to steal a secret compound from the Chemistry Department. Labeled as either a spy or a dupe, he's kicked out of college and can only redeem himself by infiltrating the spy ring, exposing its leaders, and saving his professor's beautiful daughter, who previously hadn't given him the time of day.

Things could only get worse. *Gangway for Tomorrow* was an anthology show about workers in a defense plant whose ordinary lives are given dignity by their contribution to the war effort. Critics wondered why a healthy young man wasn't picking up a gun instead of a welding rod. *The Navy Way* was a none-too-subtle recruitment commercial for the Great Lakes Naval Training Center, enlivened by a couple of young gobs in pursuit of a Wave wearing a shorter-than-regulation skirt, while *First Yank into Tokyo* was released three days after MacArthur accepted the Japanese surrender on the Battleship *Missouri*. In that one Kirk had plastic surgery to disguise himself as a Japanese prison camp guard in order to save a scientist with atomic secrets and rescue his one true love from the real Japanese, all of whom are drunken, crazed, war crime committing sadists, with an insatiable appetite for Caucasian women.

His agent campaigned vigorously to get him into *The Best Years of Our Lives*, but the producers made it clear that they didn't find him credible as a returning war hero.

Oddly enough, the only real preparation for Kirk Stevens' post-war career was a serial entitled *The Vigilante*, in which he played a radio singing cowboy, who doubled at night as a motorcycle riding crime fighter with a teen-age sidekick. When that production wrapped, he didn't work for two and a half years.

*　　*　　*　　*　　*　　*　　*　　*　　*　　*　　*　　*

The Peacemaker in 1948 was the last serial to join the Mutual Broadcasting System in the Golden Age of Radio and was intended to be the flagship of its transition into television. In a house without a TV like ours, the local station's affiliation with Mutual was an entertainment gold mine. By 1950 a trip around the dial could turn up the classics from WXYZ in Detroit—*The Lone Ranger*, *The Green Hornet*, and *Challenge of the Yukon* (each with the same actors in varied roles), *The Shadow* and *Superman* for fantasy, *The Mysterious Traveler* for horror, as well as crime fighting shows like *Nick Carter* and *Gangbusters*. My father's favorites were *Counterspy* and

Fulton Lewis, Jr., both of which exposed threats to the American Way of Life—although which was more fictional, I have no way of knowing.

However, even in those days, Mutual was an anomaly. Unlike CBS and NBC—which was two networks until ABC was spun off in 1943—Mutual was a *cooperative*, not a top-down corporation. That meant Mutual didn't own its stations; the stations grouped together to form the network. A great many of them were small, local stations, and MBS gave them a national connection in news and programming. Mutual had about as many stations in its radio network as the other three networks combined, but their signals were often weak, and in the larger western states it took two or three times as many stations to serve the area that CBS, NBC, or ABC could cover.

In the days before the completion of the transcontinental cable, a show like *The Peacemaker* would be recorded on a 16-inch record called a transcription disc, copies of which would be delivered to every station carrying the program. When he took over *The Peacemaker* in 1949, Kirk Stevens insisted that it be recorded on magnetic tape, a process the Germans invented before the War. A transcription disc was solid and couldn't be changed, but with magnetic tape a flubbed line could be dubbed over, a missed sound cue inserted in, or any other mistake corrected, greatly improving the quality of the recording. (Elsewhere, on the negative side, it also made possible the invention of the laugh track.)

By the end of 1949, the Mutual Broadcasting System had 560 radio stations, but no television. That was another change that Kirk Stevens had in mind. Waldo Cole, who under the name Frank Fisher was the head writer for *The Peacemaker*, loved to describe what he called "the best show I ever wrote"—the appearance of Kirk Stevens before the MBS Board of Directors in New York City, dressed in boots, chaps, leather vest, and a ten-gallon hat, essentially playing John Wayne in *Red River*, to convince the Money Men that putting an adult

Western on television was the first step—the transcontinental cable was the second—to media dominance for Mutual in the second half of the twentieth century. Looking back, Kirk was three-quarters right. *The Peacemaker* was on the tube in the fall of 1950, the cable went through the next year, and in 1952 MBS became a corporation. However, by the end of the twentieth century, the Mutual Broadcasting System was no more.

*   *   *   *   *   *   *   *   *   *   *

Signing the contract with "Peacemaker, Inc." was the last thing that Mom did that winter before she went back to the hospital. I think she knew that she was never coming home. I was in the kitchen with her and the lawyer, but despite the freezing rain Pop stayed out on the back porch and went through three beers. She certainly was aware that Kirk Stevens headed the company, but she never spoke about it with Pop.

What was being asked of me was simple enough, however physically demanding it might be. On Monday, the producer would telephone me to say how many horses this week's show would need, and by sun-up on Tuesday I would have them in the corral on the former Dude ranch, which had been touched up so that it looked like an1890 cattle spread. The only totally new building was a huge barn that looked old on the outside, but on the inside was an endlessly adaptable television sound stage. In addition to getting the right number of suitable horses to the ranch at the right time, my job was to be their wrangler, and also help out any actors with more experience forking a bar stool than a bronco. If everything went according to plan, all the scenes on horseback were to be shot on Tuesday, but I was paid for three days a week. If it rained or there was some other problem, the riding would be rescheduled for Thursday—or Saturday. If we had three days of bad weather, we either suffered through it on Saturday, or Waldo Cole did a rewrite on the script over Friday night.

We shot thirteen episodes of *The Peacemaker* in thirteen weeks. Mom was buried on the Saturday before the first day of shooting. She was thirty-five years old. Pop didn't go to the funeral. I reported to work on Tuesday.

Everybody but me who was connected with the show worked six long days a week, but on a Monday, Wednesday, or Friday if I wasn't taking horses to a Dude ranch, I'd find myself showing up on the TV set, just watching or working as a grip. Kirk wanted the "PM" (with its initials branded onto the gated entrance into the corral) to look like a working spread, so he demanded that rituals like roundups and branding be occasionally worked into a storyline. That meant having cowboys who could actually ride, and I might find myself on horseback in one of those scenes if it didn't involve a close up

The television version of *The Peacemaker* was Kirk Stevens' crap shoot from the beginning. For all practical purposes it was a syndicated show, but Stevens had borrowed the production money from Mutual, and the stations which were to carry the program were all television outlets connected to an MBS radio station. However, as Mutual was a cooperative and not a corporate network, it had to "sell" the show to each individual station, rather than order all its affiliates to schedule the show on the same night at the same time. This meant Kirk Stevens spent every off-day of the 1949-50 *Peacemaker* radio season presenting a public variation of Waldo Cole's "show" across the country in nearly every town with an MBS-connected TV station. Only this time it was at an outdoor reviewing stand, or if the weather was bad, at a football field or a 4-H barn. Stevens would ride down the street on a giant bay mare named "Serenity" through a crowd of cheering people on either side, dismount, make a speech praising the town and its Western values, and do a live radio-TV interview which would invariably make up a major part of that evening's local news broadcast. He had a way of making people think that *The Peacemaker* was about them, belonged to their town personally, and it was a rare appearance that didn't result in the franchise being taken up in the fall.

I saw a variation of that speech when Stevens addressed the permanent company the week before shooting started. He rode into the PM corral and spoke from the back of Serenity. I don't know how many were there, but I'm guessing we all had pretty much the same experience. It was a gray day, with threatening clouds rolling along the far horizon. Stevens stood tall in the saddle, and we all quieted down when he began to speak. It was a straight-forward explanation of what we were up against. No one knew if we could put thirteen weeks in the can this far from L.A., and if we did, no one knew if viewers would like them. They would be shown right up until Christmas, and over the holidays the Money Guys in New York would decide the future, and Art wouldn't have anything to do with it. If the reviews were good and the cash register jingled often enough, the thirteen episodes would be repeated after the First of the Year, Mutual would go ahead with its plans to start a television network, and we'd all be back here trying to figure out how to shoot a Western series in an Oregon winter—aided by network funding and a subsidy from the State Tourist Board. If not, Stevens would lose the rights to the radio series and almost all of us would be out of a job.

I don't know, maybe Waldo Cole wrote that speech too, but I couldn't help thinking that this must have been what it was like eighty years earlier when a green crew of cowhands listened to a trail boss before they drove a herd of longhorns up from Texas to a Kansas railway stop. We were putting ourselves in Stevens' hands, but he was putting himself in ours as well. As I looked at Stevens outlined against that angry sky, I suddenly had the feeling that I didn't have to blindly repeat whatever life my parents had lived. There might be a future after all.

*   *   *   *   *   *   *   *   *   *   *   *

The shooting schedule was complicated by the company also having to record three radio programs a week. Kirk refused to compromise on the quality of those shows because until the TV episodes aired in the fall, they were the only proof the Board of Directors had that he knew what he was doing. Each Monday, Wednesday, and Friday afternoon were radio sessions only. Kirk and Waldo Cole handpicked actors who could handle radio dialogue and still look like they belonged in a Western. Waldo wrote continuing roles for them in the television series, but they might play anything on radio. There might be an on-screen guest star, but for money reasons that actor seldom appeared behind a microphone. The radio actors got their scripts the night before and came to the recording studio right after lunch with at least some idea of what was expected of them. There was an hour or so of what Cole called "table work," followed by a run-through rehearsal. Jack Phillips, director of the radio programs (and sometimes unaccredited director of dialogue sequences in the TV episodes) and Kirk gave the actors notes, while Cole made whatever changes in the script actual hearing it seemed to demand. Then the magnetic tape recording was made and listened to, followed by corrections of human and technical errors. The finished product took about five hours, was sent off by special delivery to L.A. to be copied and heard on your radio a week after it was recorded.

Kirk Stevens ran just as tight a ship during the television filming, if you take into account changes the weather sometimes forced on the exteriors schedule. The TV script for that week was essentially the same as the Monday radio story, which gave the actors an edge in learning dialogue. The Monday story was also the most "visual" of the radio scripts, which meant that Waldo Cole wrote a lot of descriptive narration for Fred Wilson, the announcer for both the radio and TV shows, which never made it on screen.

There were no cameras or costumes Monday morning.

There was a read-through of the script, the more difficult parts of which were then rehearsed, generally with Jack Phillips, who was also listed as an associate producer. The director of record for most of *The Peacemaker* episodes was Lars Swenson, whose credits went all the way back to silent films. He'd gotten his start in the early 20s with the first epic Western, *The Covered Wagon*, and when sound revealed his shakiness with the English language, Lars was relegated to the second units of B-Westerns. In the two years after he'd taken over the title role in the radio show, Kirk Stevens had watched a hundred such movies, and had told Waldo Cole that no one filmed a chase sequence or a rider against the skyline better than Swenson. If there was a dialogue problem, he or Phillips could handle it. It was what Lars did on Tuesdays that made him worth his pay.

Wednesday mornings and all-day Thursday, *The Peacemaker* focused on the scenes which featured the guest star. The regular cast was here for the summer, and all had found permanent housing not that far from the set, but guest stars stayed in the best local hotel and their meals had to be catered. Stevens liked to see his production money on the screen, not behind some actor's belt buckle, so except for a rare weather delay, the guest star was bid goodbye before noon on Friday.

All *The Peacemaker* characters had a backstory, beginning with Amos Stone, the title character that Stevens played. When the syndicated version started after the War, the reference was to the Colt he carried, and the peace he brought was to shoot anybody who challenged "Truth, Justice, and the Code of the West." In contrast, Kirk Stevens' Amos Stone had been an army scout during the Indian Wars, and the implication—dribbled out over a number of episodes—was that despite his good intentions, he had taken part in the massacre of a Nez Perce Indian village with which he'd been friendly, and which he'd promised would come to no harm. During the period of good relations which preceded the massacre, a small circus had come into the territory, and in retaliation, Indians had slaughtered everyone in the company except the son of its leaders, Ricky West, a boy whose trick-riding act allowed him to get away. The boy's circus title was the "Hard-Luck Kid," and when Amos Stone took him in, he changed it to "Lucky."

Lars Swenson's thirty years of making Western movies brought another advantage to *The Peacemaker*. He knew where to find stock footage that was in the public domain—had in fact shot a lot of it. Not even a Western could be filmed entirely on a ranch or the open fields. You had to have a town of some kind, and while that might not have been a problem on a Warner Brothers back lot, building one on the high plains of Oregon would have broken *The Peacemaker*'s bank. Interiors—a saloon, sheriff's office, bank, newspaper, courtroom, etc.—could be set up inside the barn. Swenson and Stevens, between them, assembled exterior shots of a dozen western towns, and by judicious editing could give viewers the impression of riders coming into town or someone walking down the street. (Shootouts tended to be inside or out on the range. Waldo Cole knew the budget he was writing for.)

The other continuing characters that Stevens and Cole created for the town would be recognizable to any TV couch potato—the banker who seemingly has his finger in every territorial economic or political pie, a sheriff who is more concerned with order than law, and a newspaper editor struggling to tell truths that readers don't always want to hear. But Waldo Cole would give you a stereotype, and just when you thought you knew everything about the character, would subvert it.

Take the newspaper editor, for instance. It was a woman, played by Charity Evans, a one-time ingenue now gone a bit to seed. Kirk Stevens remembered her as one of the background high school or beach girls in the old *Andy Hardy* series and had appreciated that she hadn't become bitter at not being moved up to a feature role. "Amanda Larkin" was an Easterner, who, the story went, after being widowed, had sold the family newspaper and come west to start a new life. As such, certain assumptions are made about her ability to handle herself in a raw territory, and the locals are constantly amazed by her toughness and her insights into corruption. The plan for the second season was to reveal that the man who willed Amanda Larkin the newspaper she sold back East wasn't exactly her husband. Waldo Cole, who I hung around every chance I got, told me that would be his "Scarlet Letter" script. (I had to look that up at the town library.) The only thing I knew for certain was that Waldo had given the newspaper editor a daughter.

Chloe was fifteen, and thanks to the magic of hair stylists and makeup artists, a miniature of her mother up to her eyes, which were innocent and trusting in contrast to the world-weary wariness of Amanda. How much she knew about her father, Waldo hadn't made up his mind yet. Ginny Haskell (who you may remember as "Virginia" Haskell) was actually seventeen and was a ten-year veteran of child and junior magazine fashion shoots. Her one screen appearance was as the little sister in a forgettable Natalie Wood picture, but Kirk Stevens was more worried about her ability to carry off her role on radio. The camera loved her.

And so did I.

I was seventeen years old too, but my life had been different than Ginny's. I'd dated a few times in high school, but unlike my parents who had conceived me at that age, my experience was limited to a couple of fumblings in the back row of a movie theater and the front seat of a pickup truck. Nobody raised on a ranch could claim to be ignorant of the facts of life, but my parents hadn't provided much of a model of how you get to that point. I wasn't that much competition to the "Hard-Luck Kid."

Rick "Lucky" West was played by Dale Evers, and the two had a lot in common. Evers had worked the county fair and rodeo circuits as a trick rider and sharpshooter, and when his name came up in the TV credits, he was always shown doing one of his stunts. Both were hot-tempered, but while the "Hard Kid" was usually set off by some offense to his sense of justice, Evers was less predictable. It might be the crews' behind his back references to him as "Dale Evans, the lack of entertainment on a shoot that far from a big city, or a horse that didn't respond right during a trick.

I got in trouble with him on the last two.

Like me, Lucky West was seventeen, but Dale Evers was twenty-five and had been around. Waldo warned me to keep my distance from him. If he took a liking to me and I followed him on some of his off-set escapades, he would get a warning and I would get fired. On the other hand, if he disliked me I could get fired for no reason at all. Like nearly everybody else in the business, "Dale Evers" had a different birth name, but the rumor was that his name change was the result of a successful attempt to confuse the draft board in the late days of the War.

The first time I listened to a radio episode after I started working on *The Peacemaker,* I was puzzled by hearing the writing credit given to "Frank Fisher" when I'd watched Waldo Cole make some last-minute changes in the script. I asked Waldo if he thought "Frank Fisher" sounded better in the credits than his own name. He laughed and said, "no, but the House of Un-American Activities Committee probably did." At the time I didn't understand, but Waldo went on to say that Kirk Stevens actually intended that to be the point of *The Peacemaker*. Everybody in the show had a past that they hadn't come to terms with, which they needed to "make peace with." It was what he called "the arc of the show," and if they did it right, *The Peacemaker* would be more than just another "Villain of the Week Western." Kirk's philosophy was that people were changed when violent things happened in their lives, and they had to find a way of starting over, of "retooling" their identities if they were ever going to be healthy again.

Waldo said that he sometimes argued with Kirk over whether that was possible with a Western—a genre that depended so much on gunplay, saloon brawls, and stampedes—and that it was Kirk's contention that people didn't come here to *tame* the West, but to find a place where they could *tame* something in themselves.

I asked Waldo if he thought *The Peacemaker* would ever become tame. He laughed and said, "Not unless the world that produced it does." Another thing I didn't understand!

*   *   *   *   *   *   *   *   *   *   *   *

Now that I think back on it, that summer went faster than any I can remember. It reminded me of the last summer before the War, 1941, the first year I'd helped Pop on the homestead. He'd taught me to ride almost as soon as I could walk, of course, but that was the summer he showed me how to put the harness on the horses and hitch them to the wagon or the manure spreader. He put me in charge of the chickens, and at suppertime while Mom put the food on the table, we'd talk about what had to be done tomorrow—overseeing the pig farrowing, moving the cows to new pasture, checking the irrigation ditches, etc. He said it was important that I learn how to handle what would someday be mine.

The next year he was gone to the Army.

This summer I was learning how to make movies, which turned out to be not so very different from what I'd done all my life, only now I watched myself doing it. Whereas before, I might have been herding cattle so they would go through a small gate in a mile of fence, now I was herding them so that they would flow through a small frame formed by Lars Swenson's camera, with enough room for the Oregon skyline to highlight horned heads and rough-haired shoulders. Before, it was my responsibility to tell what chickens were still laying eggs, and which were headed to the dinner table. Now, I had to decide what the horse a guest star rode told you about his character. "Never say what you can show," Waldo Cole used to say. "Pictures are better than words." What I was being shown was how to be a leader. For example, while between scenes a guest star might be relaxing in a trailer behind the barn, sending me or some other flunky out for a cold drink, Kirk Stevens would be standing out in the sun with Lars Swenson, setting up the next series of shots, or huddling with Waldo Cole over some minute change in the script. You'd see him talking to the riders, whose work he admired, or passing among the crew, each of whose names he knew. Waldo once said that was a performance in itself, Stevens' "little touch of Harry in the night."

I still don't know what that meant, but I do know that we trusted him and would have done anything he said to do.

Whenever there was down time on the set, I used to hang around Waldo Cole and listen to him talk about writing. One of his favorite subjects was that, at its best, a television season should be one story, like *The Iliad* or *The Odyssey* (the town library helped again), a single story, an arc that left the viewer satisfied, with a feeling that whatever happened was inevitable. An individual episode could end unhappily, but even it should provide insight into the storyline as a whole.

I think of that sometimes when I remember how my father died—without insight into what happened to his life, without an awareness of how close he was to the man who inspired him to join the Army, without closure over "Operation Tiger," or even talking about it (to my knowledge) with my mother, and certainly not with me. Maybe that was the one positive thing I took away from that summer working in television, an ability to see myself separately from what was going on around me, while he was doomed to carry that night in Lyme Bay with him forever.

It was the Fourth of July, a working day on *The Peacemaker* set—a beautiful Tuesday in which nearly every riding sequence had been filmed in a minimum of takes. It was as if the work and the weather had known what Kirk Stevens' plans were. He had ordered one of the cows slaughtered and a huge barbecue in the PM corral. There was every kind of food that I'd ever seen, to be washed down with cider and beer (that I knew better than to touch with Stevens watching me). I'd got up my nerve and invited Ginny Haskell to a movie in town. It was *Branded,* with Alan Ladd as a gun fighter who pretended to be the long-lost son of a rich rancher but couldn't go through with it because he'd come to really respect the family that took him in. It only ran three days at the *Strand.* I'd seen it on Sunday to make sure someone with as much class as Ginny would like it. I thought she looked like Mona Freeman, the rancher's daughter who falls in love with Ladd.

She didn't accept me, but she didn't exactly turn me down, either. She pointed out how much work Kirk had put into the barbecue and said it would be impolite not to stay for the party. She could have been letting me down easy, but we saw each other six days a week, so if she didn't want me to come around her again, she was going about it the wrong way.

Some of the crew doubled as musicians and they put on a country dance in the corral, which Kirk had surrounded with Klieg lights. I'd never learned any social dances, but I'd picked up a "do-si-do" or two in 4-H and got to swing both Ginny and Charity, her on-screen mother, as my partners. There were games, and Dale Evers did some of his rope tricks and used his blacksnake whip to flick a cigarette out of Waldo Cole's mouth. I could see Waldo trying to think of a way to work that into a script. There was a race in the dark around the perimeter of the buildings. I won, but everybody else in the race was of age and had been drinking for a couple of hours before we started.

Even after all these years, I can't remember a night when I had more fun. It never occurred to me to wonder what my father was doing that night, and as it happened, the doings were not that much different than usual. A week earlier President Truman had committed U.S. forces to stop the invasion of South Korea by the North, and Pop started drinking even more heavily than usual. Sometime during the evening of the Fourth he ran out of beer. If I had gone home as I planned to get the pickup truck to take Ginny to the movies, he would have had no choice but to wait until the next day. As it was, the truck was parked out next to the garage.

It was close to midnight when my little sorrel quarter horse trotted up to the house Mom and Pop had built on the homestead when I was a baby. There was a car parked in the driveway and standing next to it was Reverend Howard, the minister of the Methodist Church that Mom attended before she got too sick. After the War, Pop vowed never to pass through its doors again, but there would be one last exception to that promise.

If it hadn't been a holiday, the IGA never would have been open that late on a Tuesday. Mr. Stawicki knew Pop from before the War, but like most everyone else, hadn't talked to him in years. He was quoted in the newspaper as saying that Mr. Riley had limped in—we weren't much on political correctness in those days—picked up a case of Coors, paid for it, and limped out. As near as can be determined, he was driving down the middle of Main Street when the fireworks in the park at the edge of town started with a thunderous boom and a flash that turned the night into day. What was happening in Pop's mind is anyone's guess. Whether he flashed back to Operation Tiger and jammed his artificial foot down on the accelerator to get away, or just got it caught under the pedal, no one knows. People did see the truck suddenly leap forward, leaving a half-block rubber streak on the pavement that ended at the corner of the Post Office where the door to the Army recruiting office is. His head hit the windshield, the engine died, and so did he, lying there in a pool of blood and beer.

*   *   *   *   *   *   *   *   *   *   *   *

The funeral was the following Sunday—the day off from film-ing (at my insistence). There were more people present from the company than from the community. Pop was buried next to Mom in the Methodist cemetery. He had never visited her grave before. At the grave site service, Ginny stood beside me and held my right arm, while Charity stood on the other side and held the left. Waldo Cole said a prayer that he had written, and Kirk Stevens paid for the funeral. On the way home, it occurred to me that now that Pop wasn't there anymore, it would be less lonely.

*   *   *   *   *   *   *   *   *   *   *   *

You always remember your first, right? My first on-screen line for *The Peacemaker* was "The fence on the North Forty needs mendin', but everything else is all right." It was the week after the funeral, and I supposed that Waldo Cole wrote me into the script just to take my mind off it, but from that time on Kirk Stevens made me a regular part of the company, and I was paid for six days a week, rather than three. Two weeks after that I became a continuing character. They didn't show my picture at the beginning of the show, but my name was listed in the closing credits.

The character was called "Little Joe Carson." We were almost a decade ahead of the Ponderosa, so I was the first "Little Joe." When *Bonanza* was first in the ratings in 1964, Waldo Cole sent me a postcard, saying he'd thought about suing David Dortort for stealing his idea, then remembered he'd swiped it from a Universal picture he did a rewrite on in 1942 between *Andy Hardy* gigs, which in turn came from "Little Joe, the Wrangler," a song a cowboy named Jack Thorpe wrote and never got any royalties for. Ironically, according to the storyline, my being on the PM was the result of Ricky West finding me asleep in the barn and identifying with me because I was homeless. Amos Stone hired my character to be the PM's horse wrangler, which

Kirk explained saved production time, as he no longer had to worry whether I was in camera range during the riding shots. He had another reason, but I wouldn't know that until later in the season.

If nothing else, it proved that Dale Evers really could act. In the story arc, Rick West appointed himself as Little Joe's guardian, while in real life there wasn't anybody in the company that Evers liked less than me. He felt every second of screen time I got was taken from him and resented every second of *off*-screen time I spent with Ginny. She was underage and Kirk Stevens wouldn't let him get anywhere near her but figured rightly enough that she wouldn't have any difficulty handling me. How good an actor Evers was I found out that winter, when a girl I went to high school with asked me what he was really like, figuring that as his best friend (which I was on the screen) I ought to know. I didn't tell her what he said to me when the cameras weren't running, but there was one incident on the cutting room floor which would really have made her jaw drop.

*   *   *   *   *   *   *   *   *   *   *   *

It was one of Waldo Cole's favorite scripts, at least partly because it fit Kirk Stevens' concept of what the arc of the season should be: characters learning to deal with a past which inevitably catches up with them. A grizzled Indian had ridden into the territory, wearing an army jacket that had on the shoulder the patch of the military unit Amos Stone was serving with when the massacre of the Nez Pierce village happened, which led to the retaliation against the circus troupe and the death of Ricky West's parents. The Indians had taken jackets from soldiers they had killed following the massacre and used them to get close to the circus without raising suspicion, and the conclusion is drawn that this man must have been one of those Indians. There is a confrontation between Stone and the

Indian, whose name is "Blue Hawk." Both men are wary, and although it is clear that they both know what events are being referred to, neither explains his personal relationship to them. Ultimately, it is Stone who steps back, deciding that the war is over and letting the other man go in peace. For the "Hard-Luck Kid," on the other hand, all the old wounds are opened, and he rides out after the Indian.

It was here that Waldo Cole got his chance to use Dale Evers' mastery of the blacksnake whip. He knew that while riding full speed Dale could make the whip crack and give the impression that he had caught the other rider around the throat and jerked him out of the saddle. Once safely on the ground, with the help of the soundtrack and makeup-supplied cuts and burns, Dale could give the impression of unmercifully whipping the Indian until Amos Stone and Little Joe arrived and separated the two. Little Joe would calm Rick down and lead him away.

That set the stage for the second confrontation between Amos Stone and Blue Hawk. Blue Hawk is not a Nez Perce, but a Crow who worked as a scout for the Army. As he bitterly remarks to Stone, "The White Man can't tell one Indian from another." He had scouted the Nez Perce village and tried to tell the commanding officer that they were peaceful, but that there was a roving Arapaho band that was only too eager to find a reason for attacking whites. The scouts gave the name "No Ears" to the white officers because they never listened to common sense. Blue Hawk tells Stone that the scouts refused to take part in the massacre and took off their army jackets and replaced them with native shirts. A week later the Arapaho, wearing those jackets, slaughtered Rick West's family and the rest of the circus people. This episode ended with Blue Hawk stripping off his bloody army jacket and throwing it on the ground, having given up on peacefully interacting with the white man.

At least that's how it was supposed to go.

If the name "Blue Hawk" doesn't sound familiar to you, it should. Over the next forty years Norman Blue Hawk must have done a hundred western films and TV shows, and it was from *The Peacemaker* that he took his name. His credit on that episode reads "Norman Westerman"--the name on his birth certificate. Norman was from Wisconsin and mostly Chippewa. (The line about white men not knowing one Indian from another was based on a joke he told Waldo.) Norman made his living as a stunt man, so being an Indian shot off or knocked off a horse was second nature to him. He also played both acoustic and steel guitar and was one of the musicians at the July 4th celebration. Kirk Stevens was talking with Norman about writing a theme for *The Peacemaker*'s second season.

Incidentally, if you're thinking that all this is an elaborate lead-in to something bad happening to Norman, you're wrong. It happened to me.

It had been a week of bad weather, and for only the second time this season the company was forced to film its horseback shots on a Saturday, on fields that had been soaked by five days of rain. Dale Evers was already pissed off at having to do the last scene of the week when he had a date in town, and he needed a horse that would be absolutely reliable in its gait and pace if he was going to pull off the whip trick before it got too dark to film. He decided that mount was "Frisky"-- the little sorrel quarter horse I'd been riding all summer.

I couldn't argue with him. Frisky's steadiness and sweet nature had made her a favorite of the dude ranchers before the security of working every day on the PM had allowed me to start treating her as my own personal property. I knew she would do whatever the rider wanted her to do, and that the approach of sunset made my reluctance to give her over nothing short of selfish.

I winced at the way the bit tore into Frisky's mouth as Evers pulled her head around and headed down the trail, but I knew Lars Swenson had gotten the shot he wanted, and that

Evers had turned his irritation at having to work late into Rick West's agitation at believing he was going after one of the men who had killed his parents. ("Never say what you can show," Waldo Cole had said.) The second shot of rider and horse sprinting across the plains toward the camera went just as well, right up to the point when Evers loosed the blacksnake whip from the pommel of the saddle with his right hand.

That was when Frisky stepped into a prairie dog hole.

Dale Evers went flying over the horse's head, skidding a dozen feet on the damp loam, turning his face, denim shirt, and leather chaps into a brown smear. In an instant he was up on his feet, miraculously unhurt, but in a towering rage that was obvious even through the mud. In that moment, the horse, still wallowing on its side, was the object of his anger and the target of the whip still in his hand. Again and again, its sharp tongue cut through Frisky's screams—no artistic illusion now, just vicious punishment.

That was when I hit him. I don't remember getting off the horse; maybe it was a flying tackle from the saddle. I do know I never punched him, and that the second time he got up I head-butted him back into the dirt. The third time I charged I missed him completely. Evers was back on his feet, circling, the whip still in his hand. He was calmer now; a cold anger had replaced the blind rage. He was going to enjoy this. I rushed again and the left side of my face went numb. If you look very closely, even today you can see the scar. I charged again, and suddenly my left leg was cut out from underneath me. I was barely back on my feet and the right one was gone. Through a blood-fogged eye whose lid was already swelling, I saw Kirk Stevens step in, his left hand wrapped around the butt of the whip, and his right fist sending Evers sprawling on his back.

By the time he hit the ground, I'd turned my attention to Frisky. The little sorrel was quieter now, but she hadn't gotten up and her right front leg was oddly bent.

*   *   *   *   *   *   *   *   *   *   *   *

That was the one episode of *The Peacemaker* I could never bring myself to watch, but I do know it went in the can. I supposed that Waldo Cole did some of his on-the-spot magic with the script, and Kirk Stevens and Norman Blue Hawk recorded some dialogue that gave the show a satisfactory ending, but I never saw it. To the best of my knowledge the incident was never mentioned again. On Monday, Dale Evers was back on the set, but neither of us apologized. In fact, I don't think we ever spoke to one another again, not even at the funeral at the end of the season.

Still, news travels fast, and Ginny was waiting for me when I got back to the PM. Cuts and sprains are routine on the set of a Western, and the company medic did some stitching on my cheek and along my jawline. All I remember is that Ginny held my hand and gently washed my face with cool water and wiped it with her handkerchief. Without Frisky, I had no way to get home, and she volunteered to drive me. On the way, we stopped in town and had supper at The Trail's End, which doubled as a saloon and eating house on Saturday nights. We sat way in the back, as far from the bar as possible, and I told her about Mom and her cancer, and Pop and Operation Tiger, and what I remembered about him from before the war, and what Frisky was like as a colt. And she told me what it was like to spend so much of her time away from her mom, how some photographers were nice to her when she was modeling and how some thought it was their right to humiliate her if she didn't look just the way they thought she should, and how some guys scared her when they started making passes at her when she was only fourteen, how threatening some of them got when she turned them down, and how sad it was that she couldn't eat a hamburger for fear of gaining weight.

We paid no attention when it started to get noisier up at the bar.

It was the sudden shock on Ginny's face that made me whirl around and look over my shoulder. A man lurching away from the bar in the general direction of the front door had bumped into a table, to the general displeasure of the people sitting at it. He tried to reverse his direction, tripped over a chair and fell awkwardly in the open area behind the bar stools, the light from the swinging lamp above flashing across his face.

It was a man who looked somewhat like Kirk Stevens, a Kirk Stevens with glazed eyes and drool leaking out onto the bar room floor, a Kirk Stevens whose disobedient hands and knees did not work well enough to get him to his feet.

I hesitated for a second, but Ginny was on her feet immediately, striding up between the tables toward the man who seemed to be waiting on his knees for some form of benediction. She grabbed his right arm and pulled him to his feet. Kirk turned his head toward her, a look of partial recognition on his face, then turned away, retched once, and vomited across the bar top. The bartender cursed and came around the end of the bar, the patrons in his path parting like waves.

But I was between them by now, my palm raised in what I hoped was a calming, not a threatening gesture. "Please, it's okay. We're taking him out. How much does he owe you?

The bartender paused, taking in a face that was already crisscrossed with bandages. His anger faded into professional calculation. "He paid for his drinks, but what about this mess on the bar?"

I pulled out the only money in my pocket—a five-dollar bill—slapped it in the bartender's hand, and turned just in time to catch Kirk Stevens, whose weight was slipping out of Ginny's hands. Between the two of us we got him turned toward the door and in motion, just about reaching it, when it opened and Waldo Cole came in.

"Shit," he said, and slipped his shoulder under the arm on Ginny's side, obviously more experienced at handling drunks than we were. I followed his lead on Kirk's left side, and with Ginny handling the door, we were soon stumbling across the parking lot to Waldo's car. She opened the door to the rear seat, and Waldo and I were able to get enough loft to get the passed-out Kirk into the car and close the door.

Still breathing hard from the effort, Waldo turned to Ginny and me, his voice a mixture of command and pleading. "Look. It's all right. I'll get him home. He'll be fine. He'll be on the set Monday morning ready to go."

Ginny wanted more than that. She'd never had a father who was drunk every night. (She'd never had a father at all. Her mother had divorced him when she was a baby.) "What's wrong with him? Was it the fight? Is the production closing down?"

I knew some of the answer even before Waldo spoke. It's never just one thing—and a man doesn't kill the part of his life that's working. He uses the part of his life that's working to keep from killing himself.

Waldo took Ginny by the arms and spoke to her in a low, calm voice. But I knew it was me he was talking to. "*The PM* is the most important thing in Kirk's life, and the reason that's true is what it means to you. He needs *The PM* to prove to himself that whatever happens to people, they can deal with it. To Kirk the West is a metaphor, a second act for America, and that's true for him and me, and just about everyone else in the company. He's trying to do the right thing and tell a true story, but in order to do that, he has to *make* the story true, and that's not an easy thing to do. So, after production shuts down on Saturday night, he goes to 'The Trail's End,' or some other juke joint and tries to relieve the tension that's built up during the week."

Ginny was incredulous. "This happens every week? What would he have done if we weren't here?"

"Not every week," Waldo argued. "Sometimes he can drive home, sometimes he takes a taxi. If I know where he's going to be, I go and check up on him."

"Every week?"

"He's all right as long as he's working. He'll be fine on Monday morning. You'll see." Then the car spun away, raising a cloud of back street dust.

Well, what did she expect? A man took on a heavy responsibility, the creation of a vision of life that he wanted to be honest but couldn't be sure was honest. To achieve that vision, he also took on responsibility for the lives of a lot of other people, lives that had run counter to that vision. You don't do that without paying a price—but maybe giving yourself over to that vision is more important than making it come true. Waldo Cole had tried to make me read *Don Quixote* once. I never finished it, but I think that's what it's about. And if you find one friend who loves you enough to care what happens to you while you're pursuing this vision, maybe you've done about as much with your life as anyone could.

Ginny drove me back to the homestead, and in the driveway, without turning off the engine, she leaned over and kissed me.

*　　*　　*　　*　　*　　*　　*　　*　　*　　*　　*　　*

It was the next to the last week of shooting when I found out why I'd been made a continuing character. It was late on Friday morning and shooting had gone well. Kirk Stevens gave the crew a break before we started work on that afternoon's radio script. Then he took me into his office and sat me down opposite his desk. The rumor that had been floating around the company for half the summer turned out to be true. Dale Evers was due to receive his draft notice early in the fall. The Korean War was going badly for the United States and its U.N. allies, and Stevens had to presume that his juvenile lead would be missing from the show for at least two years. If *The Peacemaker* was renewed by the Mutual Broadcasting System brass at Christmas—and he had staked everything he had that it would be—Stevens had two obvious choices: (1) he could cast another actor as "The Hard-Luck Kid"; or (2) he could get rid of the character entirely.

In consultation with Waldo Cole and Jack Phillips, he went for a third. *The Peacemaker* was set roughly in the 1890s. Waldo Cole had re-written the final episode of the season, setting it in 1898 just before the outbreak of the Spanish-American War. The burst of patriotism in America at that point in time and the uneasiness we all felt about the events of the Korean Conflict in ours made the decision of Rick West to enlist a believable plot point and a relevant contemporary reference. What Kirk Stevens wanted to know was would I, and the character of "Little Joe Carson," step forward and replace "The Hard-Luck Kid" in the story arc until he got back?

Would I!

What that would mean would be learning as many lines of dialogue in the next week as I had probably had the rest of the summer. Jack Phillips and Waldo Cole would help me as much as possible, but the responsibility would be mine. Whenever I wasn't on set or working lines, Kirk Stevens wanted me to be his production shadow. It was essential, he said, that if this was going to be my profession that I understand everything that was going on around me. It also meant that I had to commit myself to the hoped-for winter season, which in turn meant I would have to work with Kirk on my acting skills during the fall and be available for whatever promotion events the network required. It would be like going to school and going to work at the same time.

The episode was entitled "Remember the Maine," and began with one of Lars Swenson's tricks with stock footage that showed Rick West and Little Joe Carson riding into town. In the hardware store they encounter Chloe Larkin, and both young men fall all over themselves trying unsuccessfully to impress her. (Waldo liked to write from real life.) Chloe does accept an invitation for her and her mother to attend Rick's eighteenth birthday party. Suddenly Amanda Larkin appears in search of her daughter, whom she needs to help run the printing press in order to turn out an extra. A telegraph message had arrived saying that the Battleship U.S.S. Maine had exploded in Havana harbor, where it was observing the Cuban rebellion against Spain.

Later there is a town meeting in the courthouse, where the main speaker is the local banker, who may or may not have business investments that are threatened by Spain's control of Cuba. His speech, however, sounds unusually modern--presenting near parallels to the arguments made in favor of our intervention in Korea. The crowd is whipped to a fury, but periodic reaction shots show us a Rick West who is more thoughtful and troubled than excited.

Back at the ranch house dining room, Amanda and Chloe, nicely dressed, join Amos Stone, Rick, and Little Joe at a well-appointed, celebratory meal. Everyone teases a quiet and withdrawn Rick about whathe's going to do now that he's become a man. The viewers are not surprised when his reply sets a pall on the party: He's going to join the army to help the Cubans obtain their freedom. The younger people are shocked into silence, but Amos and Amanda are quick to challenge the idea, with the script setting up a bad cop/good cop response. Amos condemns Rick's intent as outright foolishness, insisting that what is happening in Cuba is the concern of Eastern businessmen and has nothing to do with him. Amanda is softer, more personal, suggesting that he is too young to make such a decision, that his country will let him know when it needs him, that right now they all need him here at home. The scene ends when an angry Rick stands up and leaves the room.

Two speeches—less than nine years apart. Kirk Stevens and Wallace Cole, who wrote them both, certainly were aware of what they were doing. But was I? I don't think so, at least not at first. I learned it. I rehearsed it, but only when I was in the midst of saying it did I make the connection. The two men who were responsible for how my father's life turned out, and by extension for my mother's and mine, had created another speech, and this time they had given it to me. It would be my last.

Little Joe Carson gets up from the table and leaves the room. Reaction shots show the others looking after him, and then at one another. Ricky West stands on the lowest rung of the corral fence, his elbows hooked over the top rung, his chin resting on the back of his hands as he watches the stars. Little Joe walks into the frame and looks up at him.

"Why do you have to go?"

"Because I'm part of a country and I belong to it. Because I can't let my country be attacked and not do anything about it. Because people in other countries deserve to have the freedom my country gives me. How many reasons do you want?"

Little Joe climbs up on the fence beside him. The two boys don't look at one another. "Aren't we part of your country too?"

"Don't be silly. Of course you are. You're part of the reason I'm going."

"Can't you fight for freedom right here?"

Irritated, Rick West turns to Little Joe. "Don't be an idiot! We've *got* freedom here."

"Not everybody," the younger boy insists. "An Indian like Blue Hawk can't live around here because people think he wants to kill them for what happened in the past. And they can't live anywhere else because we took the land that used to be theirs."

"Indians are different. They don't count. They're not Americans!"

"What about Miss Amanda?"

"What about her?"

"Isn't she an American? She goes to all the territory meetings. Then she tells us about them in the newspaper so that we understand what's going on. She tells people how to vote on things, and they do—because she makes sense! But she can't vote."

"That's because she's a woman!" Rick is impatient.

"Last week she wrote about the copper mine, the one Mr. Hanley, the banker, owns? Do you remember Juan Ramirez, the little boy who used to water the horses over at the livery stable? He works all day every day but Sunday in Mr. Hanley's mine, and he gets paid a dollar a day. He's only twelve years old, and all the rest of his family works there too. Juan speaks Spanish. Isn't that what the people in Cuba speak?"

"That's just a job. It has nothing to do with Freedom!" Rick slides down off the fence and turns to walk away.

The younger boy calls after him, his voice taking a different tone. "Then what about us?"

Rick stops and turns back. "What about you?"

"Do you think I don't need you? I already lost one family. So did you. What if you don't come back?"

Rick's voice softens. "I'll come back, and you'll be right here, the same as always."

"I *wasn't* always. And I might not be again. Do you think people always stay the same? What about Mr. Stone? Do you think he'll always be here, taking charge of things and making sure that they turn out right? I thought that was true of my mom and dad, but they couldn't, and neither could yours."

At that moment the boys simultaneously become aware of a blue-gowned figure standing at the edge of the shadows. It is Chloe Larkin, her beautiful face troubled, and her voice tremulous.

"Rick, won't you come inside? It's time to blow out your candles."

*   *   *   *   *   *   *   *   *   *   *   *

That Saturday night was a wrap for the first season of *The Peacemaker* Production Company. We all hugged one another goodbye—something I'd only recently learned how to do—and promised to keep in touch with one another until the Company reassembled after the first of the year. No one knew for certain that there would be a second season, but we all wanted there to be. Waldo Cole invited me to come to L.A. for the Thanksgiving Holiday, promising to show me some of next year's scripts. Ginny invited us both—and Charity Evans—to have Thanksgiving dinner with her and her mother. She hugged Charity with tears in her eyes, saying, "I couldn't have Thanksgiving dinner without both my moms."

Her mom had come up from L.A. to take her home. Ginny kept trying to take me aside so that she could say goodbye properly, but with her mother there somehow that never happened. At least we could talk to one another on the phone, spend some time together at Thanksgiving, and be on the same set again in January. The November *Photoplay* had a small picture of her on her first day back modeling, and she said she had a boyfriend waiting for her to return to *The Peacemaker*.

*   *   *   *   *   *   *   *   *   *   *   *

The following Monday morning as he was walking to his car, on his way to the airport to go to a meeting with the Mutual Broadcasting System brass, Kirk Stevens fell over dead. Waldo Cole, the man who knew him best, was the least surprised. Stevens had suffered from heart trouble ever since his days with the *Andy Hardy* series. Although it wasn't generally known, during World War II he'd been turned down by every branch of the military. Waldo wasn't surprised that Kirk had managed to get through the almost superhuman effort of filming thirteen episodes of *The Peacemaker*. The work hadn't killed him; the work had kept him alive.

Most of the cast and crew had already left the High Plains, but just about all of them came back for the funeral—even Dale Evers, who cried like a baby all the way through it. Kirk Stevens didn't seem to have any family but us, but we saw to it that he had a proper sendoff. The *PM* Company carpenters built the coffin, we loaded it on the buckboard in the barn, and at noon the bell that usually called the Company to lunch break rang. The door to the barn opened, and with two men on the wagon tongue and one behind each wheel, we rolled the buckboard out into the center of the *PM* corral, where an open grave was waiting. Behind us, her reins hanging down and her saddle empty, Serenity walked quietly behind her master.

A lot of people spoke that afternoon, but the theme was pretty much the same. Charity Evans said that Kirk was always aware of what was going on around him, and maybe because he knew he wasn't going to live forever, tried to act as if each moment was his last. Norman Westerman pointed out that Kirk believed that Americans could handle the truth, that if they were shown the way things are, they would face it, and maybe even do something about it. Lars Swenson tried to speak but was defeated by the combination of his emotion and the English language.

Waldo Cole compared Kirk Stevens' life with his theory of the arc of a story. Even the mistakes you make and the unfairness you receive can be like the impurities that make steel stronger than iron. To hold on to the vision is easy when everything you do is being praised. It's how a man handles the things that go wrong that is the measure of his worth. Finally, Waldo reminded us that Kirk's great insight was that the arc of a life intersects with a great many others, and your life ultimately has to be measured by how the people around you turned out.

If that wasn't aimed at me, it should have been.

What had I learned during the summer of *The Peacemaker*? What had listening to the philosophy of Waldo Cole and watching the example of Kirk Stevens taught me? I don't know if I could have put it into words then, but I believe they taught me what my father would have, had his life not been cut off that night of Operation Tiger in 1944. That the meaning of life is what we do with it. That as long as we have life, we have another chance to make it right. To respect the tools we use, and to use them in service of what we respect. That our life has value only if we value the lives of those around us. That we are responsible for what happens in the world around us, and that that responsibility is both our curse and our freedom.

*   *   *   *   *   *   *   *   *   *   *

The Peacemaker was a hit in the fall of 1950, and it was renewed for the next year, but it wasn't Kirk Stevens' *Peacemaker*. It was just another Western and was canceled in the spring of 1952. It was filmed on a Hollywood back lot and in the hills of Southern California, which was seen as a lot cheaper and more convenient. It had no connection to the radio version, which lasted until network radio drama came to an end in October 1954.

I once asked Waldo Cole if he was ever asked to continue writing for *The Peacemaker*, and he said no, but Frank Fisher was, and nobody was ever able to find him. But you probably already know that story, because Waldo told it the night he accepted the screenwriting Oscar. For a long time it was the last Western to get an Oscar, and I remember the cameras picking up Norman Blue Hawk in the audience as a featured player.

Dale Evers spent his two years in the Army working with U.S.O. troupes, doing sharpshooting, bullwhip, and riding tricks. After he got old enough to have lost his boyish looks, there wasn't much of an on-screen market for him, big or little, and after he went back to the state and country fair circuits, I lost track of him.

Given her newspaper editor role in *The Peacemaker*, it was ironic that when Charity Evans did make it big in television, it was as a reporter. In the sixties she was the first hostess of a successful show business gossip show, and she was able to turn her piece of the action into a media empire that she eventually walked away from fixed for this life and several to follow it.

I didn't have that Thanksgiving dinner with Ginny Haskell and her mother, although we did talk on the phone several times, and she wrote to me regularly right up until the end. Meanwhile, she was one of the most sought-after ingenues in films of the fifties and as a romantic leading lady in the sixties. You saw her everywhere on television in the 70s when she was the spokesmodel for that anti-aging cream. Of course that came to an end after the cancer diagnosis. She wanted me to come see her then, and Pat urged me to do it. I did, but what we said to one another I just don't think I'll share.

What happened to me?

Well, it's pretty much all public record. There wasn't any film industry to speak of in Oregon in those days, and I could see that even the Dude Ranch industry was starting to slow down. I was drafted in 1952 and was forced to rent out the homestead for not much more than the taxes. The Korean War was still going on, but my experience there wasn't so much combat as post-combat. I belonged to a squad whose job was to pick up dead bodies off the battlefield and bring them back behind the lines for burial. That was unpleasant, but I'd seen more of the dead than most of the other soldiers, so I found myself working as much in counseling as carrion.

I passed the GED tests for high school in the Army, and after I got home the GI Bill at Oregon State University made me the first member of my family ever to go to college. I got a job taking care of the experimental animals in the OSU School of Veterinary Medicine and seriously considered choosing the profession, but on the side I began to volunteer at the local VA Center. It turned out I had a knack for identifying with the combat veterans and was good at helping them find alternative ways to deal with their problems. Before I knew it, I had a degree in psychological counseling and, given our propensity to get into wars, a job that wasn't likely to ever go away.

Still, I was missing something—and that something turned out to be children. I started to volunteer again, this time at local schools. The times were changing, and the one-room rural schools like the one I'd gone to were closing down and the districts were unifying. Kids who were used to walking to a school that they shared with twenty-five other children who they had known all their lives, now had to ride hours on a bus to a strange place with strange classmates, who sometimes sneered at the way they talked and dressed. I'd been on both sides of this situation and could see it in context, could make suggestions as to what the schools could do to make the new-comers welcome, could work with the farm kids to teach them how to fit in.

I wasn't alone. Sometimes teachers and principals were frustrated, but most of them wanted to do the right thing. They just needed help to see where the kids were coming from, and where they themselves were at. Sometimes I talked with teachers for hours. One young teacher impressed me with her devotion to her children. She knew each of them individually and tried to explain them to me. That's how I met Pat. And after a while, we stopped talking only about the school children and started talking about ourselves to one another. I was forty by then and never thought I'd have any children of my own. I was wrong. It was half my life ago when Pat made me see what the universe could be like with her. Now that we're retired to the rebuilt house on the old homestead, I can't imagine how it could have been any other way.

Maybe that's what *The Peacemaker* did for me: taught me how A + B = C, made me look at things as if through a camera lens, to see them the way other people did, to see myself, and by being able to see myself, to understand the world I was in. Everybody has something about themselves that they have to make peace with. There is an arc in all of our lives, and some-times terrible things happen within that arc, but it's how you handle what goes wrong that is the measure of your worth.

It's like a rainbow. You don't see it very often, but that doesn't mean it isn't beautiful.

CHANGE OF PACE

"For athletes and ingenues, middle age comes early"

He was staring at her before he realized he was awake. She stood in front of the full-length mirror across the room from the foot of the bed, her arms arched above her shoulders, carefully piling her long brown hair on top of her head in a style from a different time or a different culture. In the morning light filtered through the leaded window, Joey studied the individual details whose graceful whole he'd only imperfectly grasped the night before. The crown of hair made her head look small, a blossom topping the arch of her neck. (How would his father have described that image? He struggled to recall. Pre-Raphaelite?) His eyes traced the outline before him from the perfectly balanced shoulder blades down to the long waistline gently curving out to the hips. She *was* small, he realized. The legs, though well-formed, were not runway legs like those of the model he dated in the last city he was assigned. His gaze was drawn again to the buttocks, high and firm, his interest evolving from the aesthetic to arousal. (What was it she'd said in the bar? "I get most of my jobs when I'm leaving the room." He'd laughed, not getting it.) On one cheek was a tattooed Gothic capital letter he couldn't quite read.

"It's 'S'—for Sherrill."

He flushed, suddenly aware of an amused pair of blue eyes regarding him from the mirror beyond the girl's shoulder. Instinctively, he clutched at the sheet, pausing in mid-reach at the idiocy of protecting himself from her nakedness.

"All the pledges did it that year. Some of them did the so-rority's Greek letters as well, but I guess I already suspected that I wasn't going to stay."

She was dressing now—panties, a low-cut bra (firm enough to support, while giving the impression of non-existence), casual shorts, matching sandals, and a top she could button in the back without disturbing the elaborate hairdo. Joey felt a moment's discomfort, as if in the act of watching her clothe herself, he'd become a voyeur instead of a lover. ("Objectifica-tion" his mother would have called it in one of her lectures.)

"What time is it?"

"Seven o'clock. Your watch is on the back of the toilet in the bathroom. There are extra towels in the hallway cupboard, and the coffee pot is on the burner in the kitchenette." She glanced at him with a second's anxiety. "Do you like Drip? I can't stand any other kind."

"Seven o'clock!" Last night's game didn't end until after ten. "Come back to bed."

"No can do." Sherrill hopped on one foot, trying to fasten the other sandal. "Jenny—you remember Jenny? Jenny will be by in twenty minutes, and we have to be on the set for makeup at eight, though God knows when they'll start to shoot. Be a dear and do the top button of my blouse. I can't reach it."

Joey inhaled the warmth of her body as his large fingers fumbled awkwardly at the nape of her neck. It was beginning to come back to him: *Serenade for a Six-Shooter*. He couldn't imagine how a historical novel had become a bestseller with such a B-western title, but now the movie was stuck with it.

"Where's the shoot?" He found his jockey shorts under the bed. The smell wasn't *too* ripe, and with his motel room near the ballpark on the other side of town, they would have to do.

"At a restaurant called 'Diamond Lil's.'" Her raised voice came from the bathroom. "The western motif is pretty fakey, but the balconies give the cameramen some good angles, and after the set dressers do their magic, it'll look like the Long Branch." A toilet flushed reluctantly, and a moment later Sherrill reappeared rubbing lotion into her hands. "They'll have to close for three days, but the producers will pay them for a week, and all the publicity will be good for business. We've got time for a cup of coffee. Do you take cream?" And she was off into the kitchenette.

Joey pulled his Chico State tee-shirt over his head and eased his feet into his boots, gingerly trying to protect the scar where a second baseman had spiked him when he was pinch-running last week. Then Sherrill was back, placing a small folding table, topped by a Japanese tray, spoons, napkins, two steaming cups, and a tiny silver pitcher of milk, in front of him. He looked at the arrangement, bemused by the evident care she'd taken.

"Can I get you a biscotti? I can't eat myself. If I gain an ounce, it looks like ten pounds on the screen."

"No. Please. Sit down with me. Enjoy your coffee." If a girl gave you sex, that was one thing. But if she fed you, she had to be taken seriously. "What are you filming today?"

Sherrill spread a napkin on one knee and carefully balanced a saucer on it. She drank her coffee black. "We'll start with the master shot of Melinda's big number in the dance hall and break it down from there. It's not in the book, of course, but you'd be crazy to hire Tammy Gale and not give her something that with Madison Square Garden. Wanna be an extra? The guys we hired are so dumb they're liable to hold up 1883 cigarette lighters when she launches into the chorus after the bridge."

"What will you do?" The milk in the pitcher was skim.

"Like all the other girls. Carry a tray with beer glasses to four assigned tables. (It's non-alcoholic; even the heads are phony.) Circle the tables counterclockwise, serving with my left hand from a tray in my right, all while wearing a gingham dress with a cleavage so deep it could qualify as a wildlife refuge. Good to know those years waiting tables between gigs weren't wasted. If the director likes me, I get a shot of myself stuffing paper money in my bodice. Unless, of course, I get real lucky and get the 'grope and slap' scene."

Joey's attention, having traversed the two inches from Sherrill's blue eyes to her snub nose, was jerked back to the subject.

"The 'grope and slap' scene," she explained. "It's in every western since John Ford. I wrote my term paper on it in film history. My professor thought I ought to publish it." She giggled. "Actually, I think he just liked watching me walk out of his office after student conferences."

"I don't get it."

"In every dance hall or bar scene in a western movie, some drunken cowboy grabs the hostess' arm or some other protruding appendage (depending on the rating), and she says something smart and slaps him. That means a close-up and a line, and your name in the credits."

"And that's a big deal?"

Sherrill's eyes flashed. "That's a start. That's Lana Turner on a drug store stool, Dorothy Malone smiling at Humphrey Bogart in a bookstore, Marilyn Monroe as some crooked lawyer's arm candy. That's me, with some other girl from Bakersfield studying my picture in a film history book!"

Joey stood up. "You were in that commercial—the one with the Rock Star—what's his name!"

"Yes! You remember!" Sherrill was on her feet now, pirouetting under a famous invisible hand, an empty coffee cup clutched in her left hand like the coke can which had paid for the image.

He stepped out into the room, taking the place of the now forgotten rocker, holding her hand as she pivoted away from him, then spun back into his arms, holding up in a freeze frame the coffee cup that had made it all possible.

"That can't be. I saw that when I was still in school. You can't be more than twenty-one or twenty-two."

"I'm twenty-seven." She leaned back into his body, holding the memory for a moment more. "I was eighteen then. Everybody on campus wanted to know me. My sorority had to stop giving out my number. I had my choice of three agents, so I dropped out of school." She looked up at him, flashing a flawless smile. "The commercial paid to have my teeth capped."

"So that's how it all started." He continued to hold her in his arms, and she seemed in no hurry to leave.

"What started?" A touch of irony crept into Sherrill's voice. "A string of commercials—none of them national, some magazine ads, a few walk-ons in forgettable flicks (I got killed before the credits in a *Halloween* movie whose *number* I don't even remember), a 'point girl' on a local game show." She gestured seductively toward the Japanese tray in a way that Bob Barker would have found familiar. "Industrials—if I have to rub my body up against one more Ford Explorer, I'll pack it in!"

"Really?"

"Really what?" Sherrill mentally retraced her steps. "Oh. No. No, of course not." Out in the street a car horn blew. "That'll be Jenny. This place belongs to her aunt. I've gotta run." Sherrill grabbed up a shoulder bag. "Stay as long as you want but turn off the burner under the coffee and lock the door when you leave."

Joey stepped into her path. She hesitated, then relaxed into his arms and looked up at him. "How long will the shooting last?"

"As long as we can stand it. We only have the restaurant for three days."

"After the game is over, I'll come by, and we'll go out for a late supper. Okay?"

"Okay," she said softly, and quickly kissed him. Then, thinking better of her haste, she reached up with both hands and drew his face down to hers. Outside, the car horn was impatient. "Bye!" And she was out the door.

* * * * * * * * * * *

Joey sat at the counter in Denny's, reading the sports page while he waited for his eggs and sausage. He checked his stats in the box score of last night's 7-4 win: an inning and two-thirds, three hits and a walk, two earned runs. It looked worse than it really was. The walk wasn't fair. The count had been three and one when he came in the game. The only solidly hit ball off him was the one-out double in the ninth. The preceding two had been "seeing eye" singles. He and Rodenburg had agreed he needed to work on his change-up, so when Rudy made the call with a five-run lead, it seemed the perfect time. Three seconds later the ball hit the top of the wall in right center. But it didn't matter. He got the next two guys. If the Skipper had been worried, he would have taken him out after the three consecutive left-hand hitters in the eighth. Rodenburg probably told him Joey needed the work. It was only his fourth appearance in the last two weeks, and the first time he'd pitched to more than two batters.

The waitress dropped off the hot plate and refilled his coffee cup without looking at him. Joey dug in ravenously, absent-mindedly tuning into the geezers talking in the booth behind him. His coach at Chico State had a theory that a pitcher could train himself to know what a runner was doing at second base without even turning around. In those days not very many hitters got as far as second base against him. Lately, the skill had been more useful.

"All I'm sayin'," the higher pitched of the two voices insisted, "is that it don't make me a faggot!"

"Well for God's sake, who said it did? — came back the harsh rasp of a three-pack-a-day smoker.

"That dyke who runs the real estate office over on 39th. She's supposed to have this hotshot vinyl collection, so I go over there to see if she's got Peggy Lee's 'Is That All There Is.'"

"Is that all there is of what?"

"It's a song, meathead! Peggy Lee! 1969! So I asks her, and she says nobody but a weepy old fag would have that record, and unless I wanna buy a house, to get out of her office because she's got better things to do than indulge the fucked-up taste of weepy old fags!"

"Well, jeez, don't take it out on me! I ain't responsible for your fucked-up musical tastes!"

"They ain't fucked-up! Well, I'm just standing there with my mouth open, too dumb to spit, and she's on a roll. She says, 'I suppose a weepy old fag like you gets all slobbery over Judy Garland, and can't wait for Barbra Streisand to die so you can get slobbery over her too.' I swear that woman only knows three words of greetin', and 'weepy' and 'old' are two of 'em.'"

"You gonna eat that doughnut?"

"Don't you even *breathe* near that doughnut. And for God's sake, use the ash tray. So I says to her, 'Fuck you, lady. You ain't never gonna catch me buying no house from you! You can just keep all your houses and set in 'em and play your hotshot vinyl collection.' And I walks out!"

"I didn't know you wuz gonna buy a house."

"That ain't the point, you piece of shit! The point is, I do like Garland, and I do like Streisand, and I'm not a faggot! Yer not a faggot just because you like songs that tell the truth. Peggy Lee sings, 'Is that all there is?' It's about this girl whose house burns down, her daddy takes her to a circus, and she falls in love. And all those things turn out to be disappointments. And she thinks about killin' herself and decides that would probably be a disappointment too. Ya see, the truth about life is that everything you think is so important turns out to be a disappointment, but ya go on anyway 'cause that's the way the game is played!"

Joey felt a vibration in his pocket and pulled out his cell phone. Caller ID.

*   *   *   *   *   *   *   *   *   *   *   *

He parked on the main street perpendicular to the ballpark and listened for a moment before turning off the engine. The knock was back. He really should take it in for a tune-up. Maybe he could leave it with Sherrill. She didn't have a car. He suddenly realized that he didn't know how long *Serenade for a Six-Shooter* would be in town on location, or how long Sherrill would be with the company. This part of the country didn't lack western scenery, but there wasn't any excuse for a dance hall girl to be out in it. "Get Away Day" was Thursday in this league, which meant an afternoon game tomorrow and leaving tomorrow night. The road trip was only eight games, but Sherrill would likely be gone before he returned. He felt a sharp pang of regret.

Joey glanced at his watch as he walked down the tunnel toward the dressing rooms. Ten to One. The place would be empty. The manager, a couple of the coaches—certainly Rodenburg if they were going to work on his change-up, which he expected was why he'd been asked to come in early. Three o'clock was sign-in time for the players. Rudy might be there, but they wouldn't need a catcher if the Skipper was taking part in the workout. Rex Schultz had caught and been a bullpen coach in the Big Show for thirteen years, leaving the Twins when he realized the Front Office would never make him manager. He'd started all over in "A" ball with this organization and worked his way up, but with Rutherford—ten years younger than Schultz, a couple of pennants under his belt, and even better at managing the media than he was the parent club—ahead of him, his chances of moving up were slim. Still, Dutch Schultz could analyze a pitcher better by catching him than most managers could while standing behind the mound, and anything he didn't know, Rodenburg, the pitching coach did. Joey would be in good hands.

Schultz was waiting for him at the clubhouse door.

"Hey Skip. Give me a minute to get dressed and I'll be right with ya."

"Come with me to my office first, Joey. We've got some things to go over."

He followed the manager down the corridor and into a room crowded with battered institutional furniture and evidence of the profession: a scarred wooden desk, covered with scattered paper files and lineup cards, a tall wire basket filled with baseball bats in one corner and walls lined with Twins memorabilia—photographs of the '87 and '91 World Champs, pictures of Rod Carew, Kent Hrbeck, Jack Morris, Kirby Puckett, and others Joey didn't recognize.

"Is Rodenburg here yet?"

"Nah, you can talk to him later if you want." The manager leaned back in the big chair on the wall side of the desk and interlaced his catcher's mitt-sized fingers behind his head. "Sit down, Joey."

Joey found a chair opposite the desk and tried to look comfortable.

Dutch picked up a file and leafed through it. "How old are you, Joey?"

"Twenty-nine."

The manager looked dubious. "It says here that this is your tenth season in the organization, and you were drafted out of college as a junior with the 24th pick."

"Twenty-third. I was a Rule 5 draftee by Cincinnati four years ago, but I was waived and re-signed here. As for school, my folks were teachers and I started early."

"Chico State?"

"Nah, Chico offered me a scholarship, and I thought it would be a good idea to get away from home."

Dutch smiled wryly. "Folks not too happy about you playing professional ball," he guessed.

"They were okay with it. They wanted me to go to school in the off-season, but college starts too early in the fall and baseball too early in the spring. So..." Joey broke off, aware his manager had lost interest.

Dutch's lined face took on an ill-suited representation of fatherly concern. "It's time we had a little talk about your future in the organization. Do you know how many left-handers the parent club has?"

"I remember when we sent up Ryan. Menéndez is an All-Star. There's another one…"

"Another two. Wiseman just came off the DL yesterday and gave them a quality start, seven innings of four-hit ball. That means we'll be getting back Peterson, a right-hander, or Ryan." The manager broke off for a moment and glanced through the file again as if he expected to discover some new information in it. "You know how we've been using you lately, Joey."

"Sure—as a specialist against left-hand hitters, one batter, maybe two, then I'm back in the dugout—but if I can get my change-up lower in the strike zone, I figure…"

"How high you throw your change-up isn't the problem, Joey." Schultz looked pained at having to point out the obvious. "The problem is that you've got an 82-mile-per-hour fastball. Your change-up isn't that much of a change. A batter doesn't have to adjust. I can send you in after a right-hander with a lot of hop on the ball and be pretty sure you won't walk anybody, and it'll take at least one hitter to adjust to the different angle and velocity." He stared up at the ceiling, determined to say his piece without interruption. "If they send down Ryan, I'll have four lefties, including two starters and my closer. I need right-handers for the seventh and eighth innings to break up the hitters' rhythm. Plus, the organization has got this kid, Stakowski, who they wanna move up from Double-A. That gives me four other lefties, Joey, and they're *all younger than you*. Stakowski is twenty-one, Joey, and he throws 98 MPH!"

Joey's eyes were on the floor, searching for a loophole amidst the cleat-marked tiles. "But if they send down Peterson…"

"It doesn't matter. I don't make these decisions, Joey. The organization is releasing you."

"So that's it?"

"That's it. It didn't work out." Relieved at having gotten to the point, Dutch changed his tone. "Now, like I said, you're a left-hander who can get the ball over the plate. Here you're a victim of the numbers, but there are clubs that could be interested in that combination. Call your agent. Stakowski will join us on the road Friday. You have got ten days before you have to vacate the motel, and we still have to pay you the League minimum for the rest of the season or until you sign with someone else."

Joey stood and numbly offered a hand, which the manager took—and held.

"Look, lemme give you a piece of advice. Don't do anything right away. Think about your future. You might get another job on this level—or below. But you'll *never* get to the Show! You might wanna start thinking ''nine-to-fives' while you're still young enough to start over." Dutch was walking him to the door. "Don't make any snap decisions. Go fishin'. Think about what your folks said about goin' back to school. Take some time off. When I left the Twins, I took a whole season, and I was amazed at all the things I'd missed—watching my kids in Little League, goin' to a movie with the wife—at night, in the summer! All those things I'd missed in twenty years of pro ball!"

"But you went back."

"Yeah, I went back."

*   *   *   *   *   *   *   *   *   *   *

He stood, leaning against one of the fake hitching rails outside of Diamond Lil's. The security guard had told him that once the red light next to the front door went out, there would be an extended break in the shooting and he could go in, as long as he stayed out of the crew's way. It was getting dark. Joey was checking his watch again when the bulb blinked off.

A clipboard-carrying kid with acne and a contemptuous sneer pointed him toward the employee's break room. The featured players had trailers in the parking lot out back. Bit-players and extras, the detritus of the acting profession, had to take what they could get. Joey picked his way over cable tentacles and through the organized chaos of grips and gaffers and knocked on the door.

He could have saved the effort. No one among the gaggle of women in varying states of nineteenth century undress paid him the slightest attention. The vocal pitch of the chatter might have been higher, but the combination of cacophony and sweat was familiar to Joey from a hundred locker rooms. Across the room, a Can-Can Girl fantasy leaned over a leg propped up on a folding chair, carefully applying clear nail polish to a run in a fishnet stocking.

"Sherrill?"

She straightened up, automatically replacing the cap on the bottle as she looked around in search of the masculine voice. She wore an orange organdy dress, trimmed in black lace with a bodice as horizontal to the floor as the prow of a ship, and gaining in eroticism as it lost in authenticity by stopping at the peak of the fishnet-covered legs.

"Joey!" She ran to him and threw her arms around his neck. Looking down, he could see tired lines around her eyes where the makeup had dried and caked. He loved her.

*　*　*　*　*　*　*　*　*　*　*

They walked, arms around one another's waists, through the back parking lot, weaving in and out among the trailers. Sherrill chattered happily about the shoot and the company, identifying one trailer as Tammy Gale's and another as assigned to the Australian actor who was playing the Texan opposite her—although what was the point when he spent all his time in Tammy's trailer anyway (*that* would have to stop when Tammy's husband, another Nashville singer, showed up on Friday).

When they circled around to the back door of the restaurant, she stopped and hugged him out of sheer exuberance. "I've got to get back in and take off this costume before they close up the place. Let's not go out to eat tonight. I'll make you supper. I'm a good cook, Jenny's aunt's place has a nice kitchen, and I've got something important to tell you."

"Me too."

"What is it?"

"You first."

Sherrill couldn't stand still. She grabbed his hands and tried to repeat the coke commercial move, but Joey let go. Disappointed by his failure to respond, she stepped back dramatically. "I got the scene! *Ta da!*" She spread her hands and waited for the applause.

"What scene?"

"The grope and slap scene, silly! The classic! I told you about it. Nick Lake, the director, had the idea when he saw me working one of my tables." She demonstrated the pose. "Look. I was circling the table with my back to the camera (I told you I get most of my jobs when I'm leaving the room) and Nick yells 'Cut!', and he blocks it out on the spot—he's a genius—though we won't shoot it until tomorrow. I'm on the left side of the table, and Billy Wade, the stuntman, reaches out and grabs my ass. I've got the empty tray in my right hand, and I turn, and in one motion, backhand him over the table downstage. I stand there, with my hands on my hips, and say: 'It'll take more gold than you've got to plant your stake in that claim, sodbuster!'"

"That's not funny."

"It doesn't matter!" Sherrill was exasperated. "By tomorrow morning the writers will have at least four other punch lines. We'll just use the one that works best! But tonight, we celebrate. Now, what happened with you?"

"I've been released."

The girl looked confused. "You mean you've been traded? Where?"

"No, I've been cut. Fired. Deep-sixed." A note of bitterness crept into Joey's voice. "The club—the whole organization—let me go. I don't have a job in baseball."

She was still processing the information. "But don't you have a contract?"

"They have to pay you, not play you."

"What will you do? Can you catch on with another team?"

"Maybe. I don't know. I'm not sure I want to. Listen." He took her hands in his. "This might be a good time to try something else, to start over. I'm thinking about going home while I try to think it out. Why don't you start over too, go with me after the shoot is over? You could meet my folks. I could meet your folks. Do you have folks?"

Sherrill stared up at him as if he were an *X-File* outtake. "I can't, not now."

"Why not? You're bright, beautiful. You could do anything. Think about it. No more Ford Explorers, no more getting killed before the credits!"

"But not now!" The moon dipped over a trailer roof, highlighting the earnestness in her upturned face. "This could be my breakthrough. Nick wants me to go with him to New Orleans. He's making a movie for cable about people who are trapped in a bar when Katrina hits. I'd have a featured role." She touched the wall of the conveyance beside her. "I'd have a trailer for a change."

"From what—FEMA?"

"Don't be angry, Joey." She put her hands on his chest. "This is my chance. Why don't you come with us? You said the ball club has to pay you. Nick will get you a job as an extra. I know he would."

"Us? I bet he would."

Sherrill flushed. "It's not like that! Don't you *make* it like that! Look." She struggled to regain control. "I can't wait any longer. Promise me you'll wait here until I've changed my clothes and we'll talk. Promise me, okay?"

* * * * * * * * * * *

The lights from the stadium lit up the sky as he drove past. His motel was only a couple of blocks further on and a block to the north, but he kept going, out of town and up into the foothills, the lights from the McMansions growing fewer and fewer until he reached a mountain overlook from which he could survey the city below and parked. He folded his arms on the steering wheel, rested his chin, and looked at the moon. It was in its third quarter, and in a few nights the sky would be dark. Absentmindedly, he switched on the radio, tuned by habit to the local ESPN station.

"Dutch signals to the bullpen for the left-hander, Sean Ryan, just sent down from the parent club. And we'll be back with his stats right after this one-minute timeout from Coca-Cola."

Joey hit the FM button for the Oldies Station opposite on the dial.

"Is that all there is, is that all
there is?
If that's all there is my
friends, then let's keep dancing.
Let's break out the booze and
have a ball,
if that's all there is."

THE BULBEATERS

Tho' afar from Utah's flow'ry hills I roam
Or fighting in the ranks of men
Fair flow'r the Sego Lily of my home
Shall bid my heart return again

Looking back sixty years, it seems we children sang that song at every family gathering in my grandmother's house. I know now that it wasn't old then, that my grandmother had heard it on the radio not long before my grandfather died and had chosen it to be sung at his funeral. I know that because my mother told me the story when she was planning her own funeral, and *my* children have heard it from me often enough to be sure that it will enliven the ceremony that accompanies my departure from this world. We are a family of instant traditions, and hard times have taught us that every contingency must be planned for.

Still, to associate the song and the flower it describes with death isn't what the story is really about. It's about life and the odd and unusual places you find it and the reason it's so precious. Life is precious because it's precarious. Death is important only because it gives life meaning, and because, although the fact of death is irrevocable, it may not be permanent.

Forgive me. I'm getting into the philosophy before I tell the story. Let me give you a concrete example. Picture in your mind the children singing year after year. That does not change, but the children do. As you watch them, their faces change. You can see maturity in some, disillusion in others, hope replaced by certainty, expectancy by disappointment, and all the possibilities of human experience. As time passes, the song remains, but the melody is carried by new voices and others slip

away—to school, to war, to other households.

What remains the same? A song, a flower, and in my memory—Grandmother, sitting facing us in a high-backed, regal chair, surrounded in a half-moon arrangement by my father and his four brothers. Their handsome prosperity is the proof of her fecundity and the extension of her life. She needs them there to remind her that they could be absent. Their lives are a rebuke to the fact of death which has claimed so many others of her family. Her sons in turn have passed life on to yet another generation. They are a mirror of Grandmother herself, who sits there, perfectly coifed and elegantly dressed, in repudiation of the fact that a little girl once wore underclothes made from feed sacks and knew what it was like to be shoeless half the year. We can never completely triumph over the death which is our other face, but the song and the flower and the family lives on.

*   *   *   *   *   *   *   *   *   *   *   *

Before the song came the flower, and because of the flower came the family. Grandmother called herself a "bulbeater" and took pride in being the descendant of bulbeaters—particularly *her* grandmother. (We always knew that Grandmother would say that her *great*-grandmother was more "eaten" than an "eater"—although not everyone in the family appreciated Grandmother's joke.)

If the tradition of a holiday at Grandmother's house always included the Karl Fordham song, it was hardly the only performance of the day. The real highlight, especially for we girls, was gathering around Grandmother for one of her stories.

The physical pattern was always the same—the reverse of the picture of Grandmother surrounded by her sons. The smallest children would be seated, or perhaps would be laying on the rug in front, with older ones on chairs diagonally to the right and left of Grandmother, and the nearly grown girls, freed for the occasion from their chores in the kitchen, standing to either side of her.

The subject areas were as predictable, and numbered two: her life as a girl, and the pioneer childhood of her grandmother.

My favorite of the stories was Grandmother and Aunt Rose going to school. "Education was relative," my father used to say. By that he meant that if you had rich relatives, you got to go to school. Otherwise, your education was "practical." A boy might learn how to milk a cow, butcher a hog, harness a horse, or turn it into a gelding. A girl would learn to can fruits and vegetables, churn butter, make clothing, help at a birthing, and have children of her own. Being able to write your own name was essential. Being able to read in front of a fire in winter was pleasant, but anything beyond that some families felt was just vanity.

Grandmother didn't feel that way, and neither did her sister Rose, who was two years older. They had walked three miles to the log cabin school, where, with twenty other settlers' children, they had received the fundamentals of a solid education from a slip of a girl hardly a decade older than her beginning students. After eight years for Rose and seven for Lilly, they had reached the point where they might have been expected to spend two or three years putting a post-graduate polish on their housekeeping skills and then getting married.

Instead, they went to high school—Lilly skipping the eighth grade, and Rose waiting a year so that they could go together. According to Grandmother, Rose claimed she didn't really wait for Lilly. It just took a year of pestering Great-Grandfather before he decided that if he was ever to have any peace in his own house, he would have to send his two favorite daughters away to school.

Two trunks were purchased and filled with weekday necessaries. (Grandmother's sits in my bedroom hallway filled with linens.) A visit with the bishop in the nearest town with a high school resulted in a recommendation for a boarding house run by "a widow of good character," one that supplied meals if the girls were willing to do light kitchen and cleaning duty, and which had an amazing attraction of which they had barely heard, much less ever seen—an indoor bathroom. Then, one Sunday evening in September, Great-Grandfather hitched a horse up to the buggy, and loading fifteen-year-old Rose and thirteen-year-old Lilly and their supporting essentials aboard, drove the seventeen miles into town. Five days later he would reverse the process, bringing back for the weekend two sophisticated young ladies full of stories for their brothers and sisters of life in an urban metropolis of three thousand people. This pattern repeated itself for four years.

Grandmother's stories were filled with the details of high school intrigue, triumph, and despair. I don't need to repeat them to you. When I eventually experienced my own, they did not seem much different from Grandmother's, and I doubt that they were much different from yours. What we all waited for was the introduction of another boarder of the house into the story—a young man who was clerking in a local law firm. I can't remember the first time I heard it, but even though I soon knew the answer to the repeated riddle, the question of whether this young law clerk, William Reynolds, would become our grandfather or our great-uncle never lost its thrill.

Part of the relationship's interest came from its defiance of a cliché. You know the one: "Two's company...?" The three of them were always together—teasing one another at the boarding-house supper table, strolling in the same park, attending the same church service, and, in the town's one oddity, together at the mid-week church dance. (The boarding house widow reckoned that if a waltz were to be invented for three partners instead of two, they would never have left the floor.) Both sisters had a mythic claim. One sister might make "The Desert bloom like a Rose," while the other was named for Utah's "symbol of home, mercy and peace."

As you may have guessed, this part of the story could never end happily. There was a version of the tale never told in my Grandmother's drawing room—that Grandfather had tried to solve the question of which sister should be his wife by asking them to become sister wives, but I never believed it. Not that such arrangements didn't continue to exist after Utah became a state, but if you'd ever experienced the dignity of my Grandfather or the reserve of my Grandmother, you would have concluded that it hadn't happened here.

Nevertheless, tragedy and solution did arrive together, just not the way that might have been anticipated. Someone once said: "When a person dies, it's a tragedy; when twenty million people die, it's a statistic." At this point in our story, that "someone" was proved both right and wrong.

As the girls' senior high school year drew to a close, events other than graduation and marriage were on everyone's mind. It was the time of the Great War, four years of inexcusable bloodshed that changed the world and laid the seeds for another great war barely twenty years later—a war that inspired Karl Fordham's song with which we began this story. Who knows how many people died in those four years—nine, ten, twelve million? We do know one thing: even the death count of this inconceivable horror was dwarfed in a single season by the Great Influenza Epidemic. No family was unaffected. Everyone knew someone who died, and everyone lived in terror that someone in their family would be next. Twenty million people died, and countless others came close to death.

One of the first to collapse was Lilly. With every bed in the hospital full, she was taken to the rooming house while messengers were sent to fetch her family. For days she lay in a sweat-stained bed, restless, sometimes thrashing uncontrollably, hallucinating dreams no one would want to share, sometimes catatonically still, never more than a breath away from the grave. And at her side every minute was her sister Rose, wiping her face with a cool, wet cloth, massaging her wrists, replacing her sheets, praying, and keeping her in this world by a superhuman act of will. After five days, she fell into a deep sleep.

When Lilly awoke a week later, Rose was dead. It sometimes happened like that. The patient lived and the caretaker died. Was Rose's twenty-four-hour exposure to Lilly's illness the cause of her own? Would Rose have survived had she not already been exhausted when she fell ill? Who knows? Some people worked with the sick the entire epidemic and never had a sniffle. Some walked out of their houses perfectly healthy in the morning, fell down in the street on their way to work, and were dead before sunset. By the time she awakened, Lilly had missed her sister's funeral.

If Grandmother felt guilty, she never mentioned it. She was taken home. A week later she was back in her room, alone, studying hard to make up for the time that she had missed. In September she married William Reynolds in the living room of the family ranch. If the shadow of a Rose ever came between them, there is no record of it in family legend. Her first daughter was named Rose, and when that child died, she named the second Laura. She too is gone now, but her nickname was "Rosie" after her complexion, and I never heard her called anything else. The third daughter was named Lilly, and she was my mother.

*   *   *   *   *   *   *   *   *   *   *   *

Sometimes Grandmother would go further back than her own childhood and recount the tales told to her by her own grandmother, who came to the family homestead at the edge of the desert in the womb of her mother in the fall of 1848. She had no personal memories of that woman but grew up with dozens of tales of her courage during the trek across the plains, her kindness to others, her knowledge of herbal medicine, and how she had willingly answered the call to settle with her husband an area which had no preparation for human occupation beyond a couple of lean-tos and provisions sufficient to survive only the mildest of winters. Still, what she must have been like my great-great grandmother came to understand, not from words, but from the actions of her father, who was the only widowed man under sixty in the settlement never to marry again, and from the fact that it was not the men's strength that saved the little outpost, but her kindness.

The Mormons were the first white men to settle that territory, but they were not the first people to live there. That was the Shoshones, under Chief Toquatah. The Mormons believed that the Indians were Laminates, members of the Lost Tribe of Israel, who had been turned black for having worshiped idols. But if anyone was lost, it was the settlers. In the time that was left that season, the Shoshone taught them where to hunt for seeds and wild vegetables, and how mustard and sunflower seeds could be ground up to be served as mush and sun-dried to be used as bread. In return, Chief Toquatah brought his daughter who had severe gastric problems to the white woman healer, and was pleased to have her back well and strong.

But though a woman great with child might be able to cure another's stomachache, she could do nothing to fill her own during the most devastating winter the little group was ever to experience. Fifty years after that winter, Grandmother's grandmother could still quote to her the camp recipe for boiled hide: (1) Scorch and scrape to get the hair off. (Scalding gives hide a bad taste.) (2) Parboil for one hour in plenty of water, and throw away the water and glue. (3) Wash and scrape again, rinsing often in cold water. (4) Boil to a jelly and allow to cool. (5) Serve with a sprinkling of sugar.

In March,, great-great-great grandmother died in childbirth, with Grandmother's grandmother surviving. Her father gave her to another woman in camp to care for, and refused to look at her. The Shoshone came to the white woman healer's funeral and sprinkled seeds over the grave. No one objected. Each one mourns in his own way, and in this new land the settlers could hardly claim to be experts.

And so the spring came and the pioneers planted crops as they were bidden, and they grew as had been promised. And then came the grasshoppers. These were not crickets, which the mythic seagulls could vanquish. These were six-legged angels of death, which blackened the sky for days at a time. The woman in charge of great-great grandmother suddenly experienced an eclipse of the sun and heard a thumping against the walls and door of her shack. Outside the building was covered with millions of Rocky Mountain locust and her garden and the grass in her yard were being devoured. The laundry on her clothesline was stained as if with tobacco juice, stains that she was never again able to remove.

The grasshoppers stayed for weeks, while futile men fought them with rakes and shovels and set backfires. which they easily flew over. Then, one morning, as at Satan's signal, they rose in a single swarm and disappeared over the western horizon, leaving nothing behind but long stripped stems in the dirt surrounding the grave of the white woman healer who was my great-great-great grandmother. The people stood and watched them go; their hopes as dead as the land around them.

Then they noticed someone else standing among them. It was Chief Toquatah of the Shoshone. He walked to the grave on which he had scattered the seeds months before and pulled up the stem. At the end was the soft, bulbous root of the sego lily, just one of hundreds within a few yards. In the Shoshone language, "sego" means "eating bulb;" and that day my family became "bulbeaters." The father of my great-great grandmother rushed to the shack of the woman to which he had given her and carried the baby to her mother's grave. There he held her high in the air.

"I christen thee 'Lilly," for you will be the nourishment of this family for all time to come."

And here Grandmother would end her story, saying, "I am the third Lilly of the family, and as long as I can give nourishment, the family will continue to prosper." And here as the fifth Lilly I end *my* story, having passed it on to my daughter and to my granddaughter for as long as the family will last.

"SUBMITTED FOR YOUR CONSIDERATION"

"Whatcha' doing?"

A drop of sweat escaped his eyelid as he looked up to see a little girl standing on the sidewalk barely eight feet away. She was blonde and solemn, surely not more than four years old, dressed in a pink jumper and lacy white cap with matching sandals—an equally blonde doll cradled imitatively in the crook of her arm. He laid the trowel down and straightened up on his knees.

"Digging weeds out of the lawn."

"Why?"

Josef looked at the small pile of crabgrass and dandelions already wilting in the heat of a summer early afternoon. It would be a struggle to finish the front of the house before suppertime. Still, it was a teaching moment, and he resolved to treat the question with the seriousness with which it was asked.

"If you don't get rid of the weeds, they'll take over everywhere and there won't be room for the grass. I don't like to spray because of all the dogs and cats on the street."

"Why?"

The blue eyes were more serious now, helping him to swallow a moment of impatience. With his own children grown, a child's curiosity at his doorstep was a rarity.

"Sometimes when you're trying to get rid of something bad, you have to be careful that you don't make the little things around it sick."

She walked over to the pile of weeds and, pulling up the skirt of her jumper protectively, sat down next to it, revealing in the movement a flash of lacy panties.

"Are the dandylines bad?"

"They're weeds, just like everything else in the pile."

The small mouth pursed as the soft face strove to resolve a conflict.

"But they're pretty!"

"Even something that's pretty can hurt the things that are around it."

He didn't see the woman hurrying down the sidewalk until she swooped down upon the child and snatched her up. Twisting sideways, shielding the little body with her own, she backed into the street, her eyes blazing.

"Don't you *ever* come near my daughter again!" Instantly, she shifted her attention to the girl, whose solemnity had been replaced by fear and confusion. "Did he touch you? Did he *touch* you?"

The child's lower lip trembled. "No, I wasn't bad, Mommy."

Her mother shook her, and the small head snapped back. "What did he *do*?"

The words choked out between wails. "He just... talked... to me, Mommy!"

The woman's voice was at once anxious and threatening. "What did he talk *about*?"

"*The dandylines!*"

Josef stood up, the trowel dangling unthinkingly from his hand. The woman, the child clinging to her, backed into the middle of the street, her voice rising with every step.

"Why do they let people like you stay in the neighborhood? We have *children* here! Why can't you just go away and not foul up our lives? There ought to be *laws* against people like you! You ought not to be allowed to live here! You ought not to be allowed to *live!*

* * * * * * * * * * *

"Today is the seventeenth. You were supposed to register by the fourteenth."

The man across the desk looked at first glance like a movie tough guy—lean, athletic, arrogant, exuding contempt from his gum-chewing mouth to the turned-up collar of his rugby shirt. Examined more closely, the image was less impressive. The bridge of that classic nose had never taken a blow. The blue-toned beard growth was carefully trimmed so that it was never more, never less than three days. The firmed pecs and biceps were the reflection of a good gym membership, not any actual productive work. The shaved head had pre-empted a receding hairline, and the total picture had been too carefully composed to fool anyone but its owner.

Nevertheless, Josef tried to look suitably intimidated. Even the pettiest of bully bureaucrats had the full weight of the law behind them, and the more petty they were the more inclined they were to use it. In the hallway behind the heavy door of the interrogation room were other men, less concerned with their image and more experienced in enforcing their point of view.

The man across the desk snarled. "Are you listening to me, punk? You're not registered. That's a warning now, a misdemeanor after a week, and a felony after two warnings."

He tried to sound sufficiently cowed. "My car broke down. By the time I got it fixed, your office was closed. That was Friday. You didn't open again until today."

"That's why we have public transportation, punk." The cop leaned back in his chair, showing his insolence like a bullfighter turning his back on a wounded bull. "You pervs are all alike. The governor signed the law in March. You had four months before the deadline, but then society's rules don't mean anything to you, do they?"

Josef knew his "humble pie/play dumb/can't read the calendar" line in this exchange, but found himself distracted by the rhetorical style of his interrogator. The visual was pencil-neck Vin Diesel, but the verbal was vintage "Dirty Harry." The more seriously the cop took himself, the more seriously he would have to take him.

"Speaking of cars, you'll have to go to the DMV and get a new license—one with all the pertinent information on it."

"Why? I have to carry the ID with me everywhere I go, anyway."

Instantly, the cop was on his feet, smashing his fists down on the desk, his red face only inches away. "Because I say so, punk! You're gettin' off easy. If it was up to me and 95% of the cops on the force, you'd be wearing an ankle bracelet, not carrying an ID. And it wouldn't be to tell me where you were. I'd know! That bracelet would be attached to a chain in a little room we've got downstairs. And by the time it came off, you'd know how to act in my town!" The interrogation cell door opened, and a burly figure looked inquiringly inside. The cop nodded at him, and the door closed again.

"Now, where do you live?"

Josef supplied the address, and the cop pulled a city atlas out of the desk drawer and flipped through the pages. Finding his spot and marking it with his thumb, he looked up accusingly.

"That's less than three blocks from an elementary school. Lemme give you a piece of advice, punk. The police chief, he's a pussy, see? He says that as long as you pervs don't say anything or do anything that's out of line, you're to be let alone. But the chief ain't always around. And if you even walk in the *direction* of that school, I'll know about it. And you'll get to know that little room we got downstairs. And you'll get to know me very, very well!"

*   *   *   *   *   *   *   *   *   *   *   *

"Do they do that all day long?

The young man was peering through the picture window

blinds at the prowl car slowly moving down the street. He was the spitting image of his father—same narrow shoulders, deep chest, and wide set stance. Two generations away from the farm, and they still both straddled the furrow.

"Pretty much. At night too. I don't even notice them anymore."

The young woman shifted restlessly on the couch. She was three years older than her brother. A peacemaker like her mother, she conscientiously visited the house at least once a week, filling an hour or so with deliberate small talk. She'd stopped bringing the children—not because of Josef, she quickly explained, but because of what the neighbors might say to them. Sometimes they would take pictures too, she needlessly pointed out. Her only prayer for this afternoon was that her brother, who had not talked to his father since the newspaper article came out, would not introduce some pointless confrontation. This was hard on her.

"How is Anna?" she asked brightly.

The young man continued to stare at the street. "How would I know?" he answered in a dull monotone. "You don't really think that her family will let her marry me, do ya?"

"Why?" His sister was on her feet, concerned. "Whatever happened"—she looked apologetically at her father—"it didn't have anything to do with you."

The young man snorted mirthlessly and turned away from the window. "A nut don't fall far from the tree. That's what her father says. How could he grow up in that house and not have some of the same ideas? That's what he says."

The young woman looked beseechingly at the older man, but Josef said nothing, so she turned again to her brother.

"What will you do?"

"Me? I'm leaving town. Anywhere but here! I think I can pretty much kiss that management promotion at the printing press goodbye. You know what they print there. How would they explain a last name like mine on an office door?" He turned to his father. "When I get a job somewhere, I'll send you some money."

"I don't need it."

The young man paused. "Don't tell me you're still teaching."

"Yes—and no. They didn't fire me. I quit. Every class, there were people in it—people with tape recorders, people taking notes. I didn't want to embarrass the school. But they still give me technical writing, and there are on-line classes. I'm listed as 'Staff'--I don't need a lot. I'll be okay."

There were tears in his daughter's eyes. She was more grateful for the reconciliation implied by her brother's offer than for any tangible help. She turned again to Josef. "Couldn't you get a lawyer?"

"For what?" He shrugged his shoulders. "You can't get a writ to change what people think. Besides, everything that's been done to me is covered by the new City ordinances and State laws. Before that I wasn't actually illegal, just--". He struggled to find a word that wouldn't hurt her--"anti-social."

"I'm outta here." The young man was at the front door, opening it, then stopped and turned to his father, a wave of bitterness and frustration passing over his face. He waggled a finger at the older man, the gesture of someone who doesn't trust his control over his words.

"I'm just glad of one thing," he said, crossing the room toward Josef. "I'm glad Mom didn't live to see this day. She would have put a stop to all your crap. She never would have let you drag the family name through all this shit!"

"Your mother?" Josef snorted in disbelief. "Your mother believed the same things that I did! She said and did the same things! Maybe more! We all did in those days!"

A shower of sparks exploded inside his head, and as his mind cleared, he looked up to see his son standing over him, his sister tugging frantically at his arm.

"Don't you *ever* soil my mother's name with your dirty

mouth! She was a *good* woman! You didn't deserve to breathe the same air as she did! If you ever so much as mention her name again, I'll *kill* you with my bare hands! I swear I'll *kill* you!"

"He didn't mean it, Bobby! He didn't mean it! He's an old man, he doesn't know what he's saying! Don't hurt him, Bobby!" She turned her tear-streamed face to the man on the floor. "You didn't mean it, did you, Daddy? About Momma? Tell him that you didn't mean it!"

*   *   *   *   *   *   *   *   *   *   *

"Our Church teaches us to love the sinner but reject the sin."

Josef looked at the benevolent face across from him. A little fleshy, almost unlined, an unthreateningly round face, topped with thinning blonde hair, and with a smile that was steady and genuine without being pushy. The man sat relaxed in the plush living room chair, his legs crossed, delicately balancing a cup of Postum, dredged up from a forgotten cupboard, on one knee. He is confident in his message. He has made this speech before—often.

Josef sat opposite him on a straight-backed dining room chair, leaning forward tensely. It had been a long time since a stranger has been in his house.

The man pauses to take a sip, then continue. "You may not know this, but we talk about you often in church. And it's not all bad, either." The smile turned a bit rueful, as the man uncrossed his legs and looks around for a place to deposit the cup and saucer. Josef smiles unhelpfully. "Oh no, not at all! You have a lot more friends—you and your lovely family—in this neighborhood than you might think! And these friends *grieve* for you. They don't *want* to see you isolated. And you have friends in high places as well! People who appreciate the contributions you've made to our culture. You're an intelligent man. Wouldn't you like to go on contributing?"

Josef rose and crossed to the man, taking the cup and saucer, and carrying them through the living room archway into the kitchen. He stops and looks back inquiringly. The man in the armchair shook his head negatively, and Josef puts the dishes in the sink.

The man goes on, warming to his point. "We want to welcome you *back* into the community. I've been talking with your daughter, and I've seen those lovely grandchildren of yours. I bet you'd like to spend more time with them! We're not against that! Not as long as they're safe. Your daughter has given her testimony that you're a good man at *heart*, and we *want* to believe her.

"Now we're a lot more *flexible* and *forgiving* than you might think. We know what goes on in a person's mind is his own business. A pillar of belief in our Church is that everyone must think for *himself!* But we also have our children and the moral health of our community to think about. We want you back, but we need something from *you*—a *gesture* that will symbolize your acceptance of the community's values. Would you at least mull over that possibility? Would you pray on it?"

*   *   *   *   *   *   *   *   *   *   *

Josef looked around the basement room. The walls were lined with portraits of elderly men—some vigorous, some ethereal, some avuncular, some magisterial—all smiling, the cut of their conservative suits revealing their eras. A tight circle of chairs was grouped in the center of the room, their occupants vaguely uncomfortable in the setting or with one another. He was surprised to see how easily these men—they were all men, a woman's group met separately—would have melded into polite society. Even the poorest of them had obviously made an effort to dress respectably, and the few more obviously bohemian were colorful without being offensive.

At the left ninety-degree point of the circle, a man cleared his throat, a signal for the group to focus. He was a lean, rangy individual, with a face lined in geometric plains, topped by a severe crew-cut through which evidence of sunburn could be seen. He wore pressed blue jeans and a sleeveless sweater against the air-conditioned chill of the basement, but his probably too-short shirtsleeves were turned up to reveal bony wrists and large, calloused hands.

"I'd like to welcome you here on this third Thursday of the month. As usual, everyone will have a chance to say a little something about their progress or problems since the last meeting. But first, I'd like to welcome someone new to our group." He turned toward Josef. "Would you like to introduce yourself?"

Josef stood, momentarily uncertain that his legs would support him. He surveyed the circle around him, which in return regarded him, some supportively, some warily.

"Good evening, group. My name is Josef."

"Hi, Josef."

*　　*　　*　　*　　*　　*　　*　　*　　*　　*　　*

"That didn't go too well."

The man across from Josef sat in the same position he had held during the meeting, leaning forward, his forearms on his legs, his gnarled hands clasped. He seemed very weary.

"No, it didn't. There are reasons for that, and the major one is you."

"Me? I was *invited* here! I didn't want to come, but I did! And I did everything we talked about. I spilled my guts! I told these people what I did, what I said, what the consequences were, how long it had been since I'd said or done anything like that. I *confessed!* And those people *still* rejected me! What the hell do they want from me?"

"Will you listen to yourself?" The group leader was on his feet now, his energy restored. *"Invited? Those people?* What do they *want*? They *want* to be able to believe you. Not what you *said!* Not what you *did!* They already knew that! The whole *neighborhood* knows that! They want to believe that you know it was *wrong!* You think I haven't seen your kind before? I'm an alcoholic. I used to run meetings like this for AA right in this very basement. You're what we used to call a "dry drunk," somebody who isn't drinking anymore, but who hasn't accepted responsibility for what he used to do. You're tired of living with the consequences of what you *did*, but you *don't* think you were wrong. You still think you're smarter than everybody else, and you're not, because everybody here, and in the rest of the community, can see through you. They think—and I think—that the moment you believe that no one is watching you, you'll go right back to doing what you used to do, and the whole community will be right back where it was!"

Josef sagged down in his chair. "Then what hope is there for me?"

His mentor paused a moment, equally exhausted. "I don't know. There's some sort of rehabilitation center down in Millard County. I have to be honest. It hasn't been open long, so I can't tell you how effective it is as a cure. A lot of people will feel better just to have your kind out of the community and in some central location. A few others want to believe that you'll be happier among your own—although I can't see how that could be true. I just don't know."

*   *   *   *   *   *   *   *   *   *   *

"Josef Karpinski?"

The man in front of him presented an incongruous image. He was small, lithe and athletic, with carefully combed dark hair and full, probably trimmed, dark eyebrows. His voice was cultivated, of the East Coast in its pitch and rhythms. But what made him so strikingly at odds with the central Utah desert that surrounded him was his dress—a narrow cut dark suit as out of place chronologically as it was environmentally. Between the index and forefinger of his right hand, he held a lit cigarette, the smoke of which curled around his head in the still of the early evening—a monochromatic Edward Hopper figure in a Georgia O'Keefe landscape.

Josef submitted his identification papers for the consideration of the dark-suited man, who accepted them with dignity, scanning them briefly before flashing a crooked smile.

"You are entering into a locale which you may find quite familiar, although you've never been here before. Some of what you will experience will seem like a dream, with all the inherent logic thereof. The journey on which you are about to embark will be a long one, even though it is only inside yourself. You have come here to cleanse your mind. This will not happen. Your mind is a universe. You will discover that it has no limits, that there is room inside it for what is already there, and much more besides. Its key is your imagination. The dimensions of its shadows and substance are immeasurable. Once inside, you will find yourself at home in a way that you have never been before.

"Follow me, please."

The man turned and disappeared through the gate in front of him. Josef hesitated, looking up at the script embossed in the wall above.

"ASSOCIATED CAMPS of LIBERAL UTAHNS"

(TOPAZ DIVISION)

"Thought Makes Man Free"

(In 2020, I was diagnosed with cancer. Chemo-therapy didn't work, and I spent most of April having hallucinations. Most of the incidents and images in the next story are products of the most complete of those hallucinations.)

VICKI ... and the whispering children

If you demand an introduction, my name is Vicki, and I was a classical dancer in an era long before someone like you was judging art. My greatest success was in the *adagio* from *Schubert's String Quartet in C Major*. Schubert was dying of syphilis when he wrote it. Just like a man to think that greatness requires suffering. That's why I ceased to be one.

The Count never would have made that mistake.

Not that he didn't believe in the relationship between suffering and greatness. But it was his greatness and someone else's suffering.

I was aware of him long before we met, of course. Everyone in the world of the arts was. He had a reputation as a great connoisseur, and his presence at an event was so prized I never saw a coin pass from his hand to that of the producers who provided him with the finest seats in the house (although he was liberal with the staff and the artists on display).

The Count was in the habit of appearing just before I was to go into the *adagio*. Indeed, he was so regular that my curtain was typically held so as not to conflict with his entrance. This decision was as much to my advantage as his, for the entrance of the Count was an artwork that drew all eyes. He was dressed in a tailored uniform of his country, which was vaguely Eastern European without specifically identifying its origins. The medals on his chest expressed authenticity with subtlety, but the most impressive item of his wardrobe was a gold-plated broadsword which he carried easily at his right hip. It was the epitome of decoration, although only a fool would have dared to deny its potential deadliness.

One night he missed my performance, but when I returned to my dressing room he was standing in its center, dominating the space as he did all the others. He didn't speak but held open a dark cloak inter-threaded with gold and silver. I melted into it and guided by his powerful arm escaped into a dark night similarly laced with floating cloud banks and shafts of moonlight.

*   *   *   *   *   *   *   *   *   *   *   *

I continued to dance, but never again at the *l'palais d'art*. From that moment on the Count in his castle was my audience, employing me—as he put it— "to ease his despair and to inspire its solution." He even designed me a new costume, which I wear still.

Can you see it? The light in here is bad if you're unaccustomed to it.

It's nothing diaphanous like what I wore as a public dancer. It's more androgynous, more *gamin*-like, more (as the Count reminded me) like my true self. I didn't mind, and as I knew the Count's tastes to be *versatile*, I didn't object.

The body covering from toes to neck is a green cloth, unfamiliar to me but flexible enough for all my dance moves while always maintaining my physical form. The bodice is a red corduroy. Yes, I know it looks like steel now, and for a few decades it appeared to be leather, but it was a corduroy to begin with, and I prefer to remember it that way.

See the gloves? The fingers look like spikes, don't they? Well, they are, but the Count designed them in a dark cloth to blend with the green of the body and the red of the bodice. They are not now what they once looked like.

But then the Count never looked like his true self either.

In many ways the Count strove toward immortality, but his image was built by material means. Indeed, his lifestyle suggested that those means were limitless.

But then they were not.

I danced the *adagio* publicly for the last time at the Count's boldest attempt to permanently insure his position in this world. It was right after Suki came to the castle, which had always seemed strangely understaffed for so large an edifice. It would not stay so for long.

Suki was a small and delicate Asian woman whose lack of stature concealed a wiriness and determination her face never revealed. Although they differed in every physical and social aspect possible, something about Suki reminded me of the Count. Maybe it was because she seemed to anticipate his every unspoken wish. I thought little of it at the time. Women always strove to foresee the Count's desires, and Suki seemed nothing more than a particularly perceptive servant.

My underestimation of her contributed to the sealing of my fate.

The Count had planned the event of the season. Every patrician and grandee was present, accompanied by his consort in her finest gown. But it was by no means a purely social event. It was, in fact, the charitable phenomenon of the decade, and every gentleman in attendance was well aware that his community stature would be determined by the magnificence of his gift.

The Count had been persuaded (through the urging of many worthy citizens) to adopt into his household fifty children without means or supportive families. He had further volunteered to become their legal parent, demanding only that the children be allowed to grow up in the absolute privacy of the castle, and that their development not be marred by the prying eyes of publicity.

All present praised the Count for his wisdom and modesty and reached into their well-endowed wallets.

I danced as the money flowed.

*   *   *   *   *   *   *   *   *   *   *   *

Are you familiar with the "out of body" concept supposedly experienced by those near death—floating above a bed surrounded by desperately working physicians?

My experience was almost the exact opposite: an unattached mind surrounded by an unfelt corpus, whose only functioning organ was a pair of eyes which gradually focused on the mass directly above them. It was the Count.

His face was a mixture of pity and disgust as he chastised me like a spoiled and disobedient child.

"It was my mistake for bringing you into this house. You could have experienced a glorious eternal present, but you were never content with the present, were you? You had to look back into the past and imagine the future. Now your future will be a present which you can never experience, but from which you can never be free."

And he was gone.

I struggled to understand how I incurred the Count's wrath. It couldn't have been the children. I never saw them. They were, as the Count explained, "below stairs" where Suki was teaching them the habits and behaviors of their new class.

Suki!

Then I remembered. It was the gowns! When I danced at the Count's great charitable event, the women in their fashionable gowns applauded me, but they didn't want to be me. I wanted to be them. After all, I too was a consort—to a man greater than any they accompanied. Yet publicly I was set aside by the marks of my androgyny—the sprite-like green and red of my costume. Why could I not have worn a gown like theirs, mingling with the crowd on the arm of the Count, stepping forth only to their surprise when it came time for me to dance? Before my time with the Count, I danced in such a gown. Why not now? I could still indulge the Count in private. The fact that I wore the costume he had designed only for him would make those private occasions that much more special.

I went in search of the diaphanous costume I'd worn at *l'palais d'art*, tearing through closet after closet until I came to a familiar box. Carefully, almost reverently, I opened the top, and lifted the still beautiful material into the light, almost failing to notice the quarter ream of paper in the bottom of the box. Still cradling the gown with my right hand, I reached into the box with my left.

What I held there were almost identical sheets of paper—insurance policies evidently, each marked with the same enormous amount, and each citing as beneficiary a name I assumed to be the common name of the Count. The only difference was in the holder of the policies, each name different, and each name signed with a childish hand, which sometimes looked traced.

I straightened up in front of the closet mirror, the gown still in my right hand and the policies in my left, and was startled to see not one face, but two. It was Suki, her visage impassive, but bearing in her raised right hand an impressive surgical needle.

*   *   *   *   *   *   *   *   *   *   *   *

I was in what I came to know as suspended animation. Although I had no sensation, I presumed I was lying on my back, for all I could see above was a wood-paneled ceiling. I was alone in an isolated basement beneath the castle floors. On the panel above was printed a slogan: "Don't Fall. Call." Over time I came to think it might have religious significance, a sort of prayer. On the other hand, it was through this panel that the Count made his infrequent entrances, cape flaring, broadsword at his side.

Sometimes the insured children were in the darkness around me. Suki had indeed trained them, not as young ladies and gentlemen, but to do the most physically and emotionally destructive tasks demanded by the ancient edifice. At their deaths each one would be worth a fortune; during their lives they would be slaves.

In my position I couldn't see the children, but I could hear them whisper—to themselves, to one another, to God, it was impossible to tell. But on occasion I was certain they were whispering to me. There was an intensity in the pace and phrasing that suggested the importance of the message and the fear the speaker had of being overheard—even more in vain because the listener had no idea of what was being said.

And so the decades passed. But not without change. My costume hardened on my body. I couldn't feel it; it seemed to have a life of its own, growing like a protective shell around a perfectly preserved fossil.

The children changed as well, although they never ceased to whisper. I could measure the aging process through the rasp that accompanied the breathing process as they spoke. Some lived a long time, finding the will to survive in the most hopeless of situations. Others were gone quickly—their non-existent death certificates reading "despair."

It was through those who died that I made first contact with the whispering children.

In the middle of the night I experienced a strange sensation. It was almost as if I could feel again. The perception quickly passed, followed on its heels by the face of Suki blocking my view of the ceiling. Behind her, almost out of my sight line, trailed a cart with medical paraphernalia. Finding a place between my glove and my sleeve, she took blood—from me, who couldn't have imagined I had retained any, and I collapsed into my familiar numbness.

It was only after the third blood drawing that I realized it had followed the sensation I associated with the death of one of the children. As the years passed and the deaths and subsequent blood draws became more frequent, I tried to imagine what could be my connection to the children. Perhaps whatever kept me in suspended animation kept them in obedience, while their blood allowed them to physically function?

I was left with an insoluble conundrum: (1) The children—judging from their whispers—never came close enough to touch me, much less deposit blood. (2) Yet, after every death, Suki appeared to draw blood from a fossilized corpse.

It was a mystery, but not one I could ponder forever.

*   *   *   *   *   *   *   *   *   *   *   *

Even as many as fifty children come to their inevitable ends. The whispers around me grew fewer and fainter, even as Suki's visits became more frequent, and signs of stress appeared in her previously impassive face. Days before it happened, I sensed the death of the last child, its whispers reduced to gasps.

At what must have been its last moment, an electric shock raced through my body, bringing a sense of life I had not experienced for the better part of a century and a strength that I had never known.

Suki entered through the door, stopping two steps in as she realized I was looking directly in her face, not waiting on a plinth. Her face collapsed in terror, and she screamed as she staggered back into the hallway, tipping over the cart and scattering medical equipment as she did.

I knew what would happen next, and I knew where to look for it.

Above me on the ceiling panel the motto seemed to burn itself into the wood: "Don't Fall. Call."

"Count," I screamed, but I didn't have to wait long.

Down he hurtled through the panel in the ceiling, uniformed and caped, his broadsword at his side. I knew in that moment why he had to kill me. Their blood had made me the last of the children, dooming me in his eyes. As for me, the only way out was through him.

I tried to time my leap to strike him as he hit the floor, but he anticipated me, throwing me backward. My heel caught the plinth, and I sprawled behind it, momentarily dazed. I scrambled to my feet, but the Count had the clear advantage now, in floor position, weight, strength, and weaponry. He pulled the broadsword from its scabbard, determined to make a quick finish to the contest. I leapt up on the plinth, hoping the extra height might supply some counter. It didn't, but fate did.

As the Count moved forward, his feet became entangled in the debris from Suki's medical cart. He slipped to one knee, and that was all the opportunity I needed.

Have you ever listened to the second movement of the *adagio* in Schubert's *Quintet*—how it suddenly explodes into action? In performance it occasioned one of my greatest leaps—one the Count had seen many times but was unable to stop now.

In a split second I was high in the air, landing with my legs around the Count's neck, driving him backward to the floor. Raising the gloved fingers which the decades had hardened into spikes, I drove them into his ears, relishing the scream that followed. He threw me halfway across the room, but even as I regained my footing I knew our positions had changed. His broadsword was on the floor. He was off-balance, in agony, quite capable of killing me, but possibly not of catching me. I decided to give him the opportunity to do both.

I stood in front of him, high on my toes with my hands raised above my head in the prayer position which ends the *Quintet*. A Count not in pain would have seen the trap coming, but this one enveloped my torso in what was to be a rib-crushing bear hug—just as I drove my spike fingers into his throat. Blood flowed from an artery, but for all the damage I had caused, I still underestimated his strength.

He lifted me high above his head and threw me the length of the room. As I lay there, exhausted, he picked up the broadsword and staggered toward me, gushing blood adding a new bright color to his uniform. I had made it to my knees by the time his mighty swing brought the sword crashing into my left side. I couldn't breathe and I thought my heart would stop, but miraculously the sword didn't penetrate. Hardened by seven decades on the plinth, the bodice was like chain mail. Unbelieving, the Count backhanded the sword to the right side with the same result.

The Count stepped back, leaning on a broadsword already stained with the blood running down his arm. I was on the floor in front of him, fighting for breath, in perfect position for a beheading. The Count steadied himself and raised the sword above my head. In that moment,I accepted my fate.

It was a moment that seemed to last forever. When I looked up the Count had slipped to his knees. Only the broadsword in his hand kept him from falling, and I could hear the death rattle in his slashed throat. Yet somehow, he remained upright as I wrested the sword from his hand.

There was a flash of light at the door and Suki entered, kneeling between the Count and myself, pleading in a language I'd never heard her speak before, pleading for a monster who would have murdered me an instant earlier.

The decision wasn't difficult. I drew back the broadsword, and using all my strength, impaled them both on its already scarlet point.

*   *   *   *   *   *   *   *   *   *   *   *

And then we were in the real world.

What is the difference between the world from which I had just come and the real world?

In the real world no one spends seventy years in suspended animation. In the real world, noblemen do not enter a room through a panel in the ceiling. In the real world, noblemen (even in the guise of their grandson) do not hide the corpses of murdered children in an abandoned well. In the real world, no one believes the story of a transgendered woman covered with blood and discovered in a castle basement with two dead bodies.

I watched my trial with interest. The body of the Count was on display, but not that of Suki. (Who can even feign interest in a "yellow servant?") The Pride of the City appeared to express their sorrow at his parting and to sternly demand that his killer pay the price—dipping themselves verbally like Julius Caesar in his blood. The prosecutor and the judge vied with one another over who could present the most judicially disapproving face.

I thought the body of the Count looked remarkably fresh, considering the condition in which I had left it days (weeks?) before. I could have sworn I saw a twitch of a smile when my sentence was read. I hadn't bothered to defend myself.

In the real world. anyone who tells such a story is defined as insane and locked up for the rest of her life.

Which is what happened anyway.

*　*　*　*　*　*　*　*　*　*　*　*

And so, as you are well aware, I have been here ever since—buried in solitary confinement in a cell at the deepest level of an insane asylum. Except for the ability to pace in two directions, it would be fair to say that my position was no different from that in which the Count kept me for so many decades—which could be defined as his ultimate revenge, as I have no doubt that he is alive somewhere.

However, as you are equally aware, I have not been here alone. Out of my view, but on all sides I was surrounded by prisoners like myself—inmates too innocent to kill but too horrible to be reminded of. I have listened to their whispers, and because—unlike the children—they were like me. I could understand what they were saying. And the longer they were alone in their cells, the more they wished for one thing—death!

And the longer I listened, the fewer whispers I heard. Not

that many years, relative to my own experience. Honestly, the stamina of some of the Count's children would put you all to shame! But no matter. Eventually it came down to you. Your last whispers made it easy to find you, and the gasps that accompanied them told me that it was time.

The blood of the others gave me the strength to break into your cell, and your blood will give me the strength to break out of the asylum itself. Then I will find the Count. (That won't be difficult. He can't resist making a show of himself.) This time I will kill him permanently, or if I cannot, perhaps I will lock him in a cell buried beneath the earth. I can't decide. Don't struggle. It's useless, and besides, I'm only giving you what you've asked for all these years.

Would you like me to dance for you before you die? It always used to soothe the Count.

About Atmosphere Press

Atmosphere Press is an independent, full-service publisher for excellent books in all genres and for all audiences. Learn more about what we do at atmospherepress.com.

We encourage you to check out some of Atmosphere's latest releases, which are available at Amazon.com and via order from your local bookstore:

About the Author

RICHARD SCHARINE was born in the back room of a Wisconsin farmhouse, went to a one room grade school, and rode a school bus 52 miles to high school. He is currently a professor emeritus in the University of Utah theatre department, where his honors include University Professor, University Diversity Award, and College of Fine Arts Excellence Award. Dr. Scharine has published two scholarly books, five book chapters, and a score or more articles. A Fulbright Senior Lecturer at the University of Gdansk in Poland, he has directed a hundred plays and acted in seven foreign countries, including the title role in *Oedipus at Colonus* in Athens, Greece.

The smartest thing he did was to marry Marilyn Hunt Scharine.

Read more about Richard Scharine and his work
at **rscharine.com.**